The Bargaining Book

A Guide to Collective Bargaining in the Federal Government
5th Edition

by Philip A. Varnak

Published by:
FPMI • 4901 University Square, Suite 3
Huntsville, AL 35816
(256) 539-1850 • Fax: (256) 539-0911

Internet Address:
http://www.fpmi.com • e-mail: fpmi@fpmi.com

Table of Contents

The • Bargaining • Book

FPMI
Star Mountain, Inc.
© 2003

Table of Contents

FPMI
Star Mountain, Inc.
© 2003
The • Bargaining • Book

Introduction

Good negotiators are made — not born. If you have been selected by your agency or your union to participate on a bargaining team, you may not have had any experience in labor negotiations. In many respects, however, labor negotiations are not any different than negotiating on the price of a car or a piece of furniture. As a result, you are bringing with you a good deal of experience. In all negotiations, the goal is basically the same–to reach an agreement that both sides voluntarily accept.

This book is specifically designed for negotiators tasked with reaching agreement on a contract between management and labor in the federal government. Many of the rules, regulations, and procedures that govern the conduct of Federal sector negotiations are unique. *The Bargaining Book* will show you how to use your practical experience and how to work within the requirements unique to the Federal system.

This book covers the requirements that are essential to successfully negotiating a collective bargaining agreement or an agreement being negotiated during the existing term of a basic agreement. It is designed to enable you to read and absorb the information at your own pace. It can be used as a self-contained document, as a reference book, or in conjunction with a program of formal instruction.

The book is based on Title VII of the Civil Service Reform Act of 1978. It has been divided into units within each chapter to enable you to better understand the stages of the bargaining process through which most negotiations will progress. Each chapter builds on the information contained in the previous portions of the book.

In 1993, President Clinton signed Executive Order 12871 that implemented a period of Labor Management Partnerships within the Federal Sector. This Executive Order did not amend Title VII of the CSRA but rather emphasized some flexibility contained within the Statute that most Federal agencies had opted not to utilize. Even though President Bush rescinded that Executive Order in 2001, the concepts set forth by EO 12871 continue to live since they are fully permitted under Title VII. Throughout this book, we will address the concepts and how they continue to be applied in the Federal Sector.

The Bargaining Book is not intended to make you an expert in the field of federal sector labor relations. If you need more information on the basic concepts of the program, you

FPMI
Star Mountain, Inc.
© 2003

may want to read *The Supervisor's Guide to Federal Labor Relations* or *The Union Representatives Guide to Federal Labor Relations,* published by FPMI Communications, Inc.

Each segment of information is presented as a statement of fact and immediately following the information, you will be asked to answer one or more questions requiring the application of these facts. This example illustrates the structure used throughout the book:

Information: Title VII of the Civil Service Reform Act entitles employees to form, join or assist a labor union or to refrain from doing so.

Question: An employee you supervise wants to join a union. You believe it would affect the productivity and efficiency of your office. Can you attempt to persuade the employee not to join the union?

ANSWER

A. Yes, because a union does not have the right to affect the productivity of federal employees.

B. No, because each employee has been given this right under the labor relations statute.

C. Yes, because the right of employees to organize a union does not exist until an election has been conducted.

In this case, the correct answer is B. You should circle that letter. B is the correct answer because, based on the facts presented in the information first given to you, an employee has the right to form a union and a supervisor cannot interfere with that right. Throughout this book, the correct answer and an explanation of that answer will immediately follow.

For consistency and ease in learning, the same characters are used throughout *The Bargaining Book*. By the time you have finished this course, you will feel like you know them quite well. *Mary Jamison* is the Chief Negotiator for the agency's bargaining team. *Sam McLean* is the Chief Negotiator for the union's team.

As is typical of most people who engage in their first contract negotiations, both Mary and Sam have a great deal of common sense on which to draw, but have not had much experience in negotiating under the rules and requirements of the federal labor relations program.

As you progress through this course, you will benefit from their experiences and will learn to avoid some of their mistakes in your own negotiations.

Introduction

"Should I use traditional bargaining techniques or other methods such as interest based bargaining (IBB)?" Executive Order 12871 encourages the use of processes such as IBB and our experience has been that it works well in many situations.

The final decision of what method to use is up to the parties to the bargaining process. You are likely to find that traditional bargaining will still be necessary in some situations and depending on the nature of the labor relationship may actually be used for an entire contract. Others will rely largely on interest-based bargaining.

We have covered both methods in this, the fourth edition of *The Bargaining Book*. Regardless of which method you choose, preparation and hard work are still necessary.

Remember to take as long as you need to study and understand the material. If necessary, return to previous chapters to review the subject matter before going on.

A number of changes have been made in this edition to provide more comprehensive coverage of the bargaining process in the federal government. Many changes were the result of suggestions made by those who read and used the first editions of the book. Please send your comments and any suggestions to FPMI Communications, Inc.

FPMI
Star Mountain, Inc.
© 2003

Bargaining · Basics

Chapter 1

FPMI
Star Mountain, Inc.

FPMI
Star Mountain, Inc.
© 2003

The · Bargaining · Book

Bargaining Basics

I have used the term "bargaining basics" to describe the concepts and principles with which you must be familiar in order to be a successful negotiator. Bargaining basics directly influence all federal labor negotiations. Successfully representing your agency or your union requires you to be knowledgeable about the basic concepts of the federal program before participating in the dynamics of the bargaining process. After reading this chapter, you will know:

• How to define a bargaining unit.

• When a union becomes the representative of employees.

• Who is represented by a union.

• The categories of employees excluded from a bargaining unit.

• The difference between a unit member and a union member.

The Bargaining Unit

The bargaining unit is a group of employees with common interests: A unit is:

• Designated by the Federal Labor Relations Authority (FLRA).

• Represented by a Union.

1. Mary Jamison is the Chief Negotiator for the management negotiating team. The union gives her team a proposal to exclude all wage grade employees from the bargaining unit. She knows that these employees have been included in the unit for a number of years. Should she agree to this proposal?

A. Yes, but only if the management team believes that the wage grade employees have common interests with the remainder of the unit.

B. No, because only the FLRA can alter the categories of employees that are in a bargaining unit.

C. Yes, but only if the union will agree to a written understanding that the two parties (management and the union) have both agreed to the new unit description.

ANSWER

1. The agency and the union do not have the authority under the labor relations statute to determine the categories of employees that are in or out of the bargaining unit. If they jointly determine that the unit should be changed by excluding the wage grade employees, either management or the union (or both) can file a petition with the Federal Labor Relations Authority to have the unit altered. It is also possible for the contract to contain contract articles applicable only to the wage grade employees when that is desirable.

In all probability, if both management and the union agree to certain unit exclusions, the agreement will never be challenged. However, any challenge that is filed by any affected party is almost certain to be resolved by retaining the unit structure until the FLRA has approved a change. Good judgment requires that such an informal arrangement not be agreed upon at the bargaining table.

For these reasons, the correct answer to this question is B.

QUESTIONS

2. Prior to the start of the negotiations, the local union president, Sam McLean, collected the signatures of forty percent of all employees in an organization he would like the union local to represent. He presented these signatures to the personnel officer for the agency employing those who signed the petition and stated he would like to open contract negotiations in the next two weeks. What would an appropriate response from the personnel officer be?

The Union

The union becomes the employees' representative after an election and certification by the FLRA. The union:

• Represents all unit employees.

• Must represent all employees equally.

• May negotiate an agreement with agency management.

    A. Since the union collected the signatures of more than thirty percent of the bargaining unit, it is proper to begin negotiations. He should assemble a bargaining team to begin bargaining preparations.

B. The union is only entitled to negotiate on behalf of the forty percent of the employees that have signed the petition. He should inform the local president of this and agree to negotiate an agreement on behalf of those employees only.

C. The union cannot be considered as the representative of the employees in the unit until an election has been conducted. The personnel officer should not consider the union's request to bargain until the FLRA has conducted an election and certified the results.

3. After Certification of the Union by FLRA and the start of negotiations, Sam McLean submits a proposal stating that the union will represent only dues paying members of the union. The proposal also states that employees who are not members of the unit are free to secure their own representative since they have not elected to take advantage of the union's services. Should the agency consider this offer?

A. Yes, because the issue is one of internal union business only and should not concern the agency.

B. Yes, because the union should not have to represent employees who are not willing to pay their fair share of the union's expenses.

C. No, because the union has an obligation to represent all employees in the unit equally without regard to union membership.

NOTES

The•Bargaining•Book

FPMI
Star Mountain, Inc.
© 2 0 0 3

ANSWERS

2. Management and the union cannot negotiate a labor agreement until an election has been conducted and the results have been certified by the Federal Labor Relations Authority (FLRA). While the union has met the requirements for submitting a petition for an election, it does not become the representative of the employees in the bargaining unit until certification by the FLRA. *The correct answer is C.*

3. The union has an obligation to represent all employees in the bargaining unit equally without regard to membership in the union. While on the surface this would appear to be a matter affecting only the internal business of the union, management also has an obligation to ensure that the provisions of the labor relations statute are met. In this case, an employee who was not a member of the union could file a valid complaint against both the agency and the union for restricting his right to union representation if the agency agreed to this proposal. *Therefore, the correct answer is C.*

Bargaining Unit Exclusions

Some categories of employees are always excluded from a bargaining unit. These are:

- Management Officials

- Supervisors

- Confidential Employees

- Personnelists (other than clerical)

- Certain Employees Engaged in Security Work

4. Sam McLean is the Chief Negotiator for the Union's bargaining team. One other member of his team wants to negotiate a contract provision covering the rights of all supervisors in the agency. The agency's team has refused to consider any proposal that covers supervisors. What action should Sam take now?

A. He should insist on the provision being included in the contract because it would be good for the morale of the supervisors.

B. He should explain to the team member who wants to negotiate the provision that the agreement can only cover employees in the bargaining unit and, since supervisors are not in the unit, the union does not have the right to represent them.

C. He should file a negotiability appeal or an unfair labor practice charge with the Federal Labor Relations Authority in order to preserve the rights of the union.

5. Mary Jamison's team has proposed that all secretaries working for a second level supervisor or higher be excluded from the coverage of the collective bargaining agreement. What should Sam's answer be?

A. The proposal should be rejected by the union because there is no basis for excluding all secretaries in the agency just because they work for a second level supervisor. Therefore, Sam should insist that all secretaries in the agency remain in the bargaining unit.

B. As all confidential employees are excluded from the bargaining unit, the agency's proposal is consistent with the law and must be accepted.

C. Sam should agree with the agency to exclude only those secretaries that have access to confidential labor relations information. He should not agree to exclude all secretaries above the second level of supervision as it would improperly take employees out of the bargaining unit.

FPMI
Star Mountain, Inc.
© 2003

ANSWERS

4. The union only represents employees in the bargaining unit. It cannot represent or negotiate a contract for any other employees. As noted in the information at the beginning of this section, supervisors are outside the bargaining unit and cannot be represented by the union.

Filing an appeal with the FLRA to determine the negotiability of the proposal would be futile for this reason. Likewise, filing an unfair labor practice against the agency would be a waste of time and unnecessarily delay the negotiations. *The correct answer is B.*

5. Insisting that all secretaries remain in the bargaining unit would not be proper as some of them may be confidential employees. A confidential employee is defined by the Federal Labor Relations Authority as a person who uses confidential labor relations information in the performance of his or her duties. This definition is unlikely to cover all secretaries encompassed by the agency's proposal. In order to maintain the integrity of the bargaining unit, the union should agree to exclude only those secretaries that are truly confidential employees. *The correct answer is C.*

QUESTIONS

6. During negotiations, Sam proposes that the contract article on the negotiated grievance procedure only be available to the 40 percent of the employees who have elected to become members of the union. Under this proposal, the other 60 percent of the bargaining unit will have to use the agency grievance procedure or any applicable statutory appeal procedure. Is this proposal compatible with the labor relations statute?

Unit and Union Membership

- Any employee may pay dues to the union

- Union members are not represented by a union unless they are in the unit

- The union represents all employees in the unit

- Unit employees are represented by the union even if they do not pay dues

---

    A. No, because a union must represent all members of the unit equally. It cannot distinguish between union members and unit members.

    B. Yes, because the union is only obligated to represent those employees that share the union's expenses by paying membership dues.

    C. Yes, because the proposal concerns internal union business and management cannot attempt to influence how the union is managed.

7. A supervisor files a grievance with agency management. In his grievance, he indicates that he pays dues to the Union and wishes to file the grievance under the provisions of the union contract. Should management allow the supervisor to use the grievance procedures of the union agreement?

    A. Yes, but the union cannot represent him because it would be a conflict of interest.

    B. No, because he is not a member of the bargaining unit and the agreement does not apply to him.

    C. Yes, but only if he is a dues paying member of the union and has paid for the right to use the agreement.

8. This supervisor was previously a bargaining unit member before being promoted to his current position. The Labor Relations Specialist verifies that he is still having dues deducted from his pay. The LR Specialist should:

    A. Do nothing because the supervisor was previously a bargaining unit member.

    B. Discontinue the payroll deductions because payroll deductions are only available for current bargaining unit members.

    C. Do nothing because anyone can join the union and that membership entitles him to payroll deductions.

NOTES

The•Bargaining•Book

FPMI
Star Mountain, Inc.
© 2003

ANSWERS

6. A union must represent *all* employees in the unit equally. It cannot make distinctions regarding coverage of the contract between dues paying members and non-dues paying members of the bargaining unit. Management would also be committing an unfair labor practice if it acquiesced to the union's proposal. *The correct answer is A.*

7. A negotiated grievance procedure is part of a collective bargaining agreement. Consequently, the right to use it belongs only to the members of the bargaining unit. A supervisor cannot use the grievance procedure as he cannot, by definition, be a member of a bargaining unit. Management could, if it wished, establish an agency grievance procedure similar to the procedure contained in the agreement for all employees outside the bargaining unit and, in fact, many of them have done so. (These agency procedures do not contain an arbitration procedure, however.) *The correct answer is B.*

8. Any employee of the agency may join a union including supervisors and managers. However, unless the employee is in a bargaining unit position, he/she is not entitled to have dues deducted by payroll deduction. An employee not in a bargaining unit position would pay dues directly to the union. *The correct answer is B.*

FPMI
Star Mountain, Inc.
© 2 0 0 3

Getting • Started

Chapter 2

FPMI
Star Mountain, Inc.

The • Bargaining • Book

Getting Started

Like any successful project, knowing where to start is important. This chapter will show you how to begin preparing for your negotiations. Discipline yourself to follow these initial steps. Your negotiations will proceed smoother, faster and your prospects of achieving your goals will be greater.

If you yield to the temptation of skipping the preparation process, you are likely to find yourself with an agreement that does not meet your needs or objectives. If you are going to negotiate, face the inevitable. Effective bargaining requires a lot of hard work. At the end of the negotiations, most negotiators, with the benefit of hindsight, prefer the hard work and preparation required to do a good job before sitting down to the bargaining table, to the embarrassment, frustration and confusion that will result when a poor agreement is reached.

After reading this chapter, you will understand:

- The nature and role of the preparation team.

- Guidelines for bargaining team selection.

- The structure and function of a bargaining book.

- How to effectively prepare for negotiations.

Preparation Team

- A preparation team will:

- Study the current agreement to identify problem articles

- Analyze grievances

- Review contracts in other installations

- Review arbitration decisions

- Analyze economic data

QUESTIONS

9. In preparing for negotiations, Mary Jamison is attempting to decide what objectives she wants to achieve in the new contract. To do this, she intends to involve all levels of management. When she looks at people to assist her, she has a total of fifteen. Her boss questions her judgment for involving that many. How should she respond?

FPMI
Star Mountain, Inc.
© 2 0 0 3

A. The preparation team serves a different function than the bargaining team. It should represent all major components of the agency and may be larger than the negotiating team. Increasing its size may make the negotiating team and the final agreement more acceptable to the entire organization.

B. The preparation team should be much smaller than fifteen people and she should review the list to make it smaller.

C. She should only have the members of the negotiating team handle all preparations.

10. In preparing proposals, Mary is wondering what factors she should consider. Which of the following considerations should be important to her?

A. Potential expenses and benefits

B. Whether other agencies have negotiated on the same subject

C. Whether a subject is within the bounds of the labor relations statute.

D. All of the above.

11. Sam asks one of his preparation team members to analyze the cost of running a day care center since the union is considering making a proposal on this issue. The team member asks him why he needs that since they know their members want it anyway and it will require a lot of time and effort. What should Sam tell his team member?

A. If the union can really prove that its members want the day care center, the economic data is not necessary.

B. If the union is serious about getting agreement on a day care center, a thoroughly researched proposal showing the amount of money needed to run the operation and a plan for raising the money will be more acceptable to the management team and is likely to be more successful when implemented.

C. Sam should ask someone else to do the work.

FPMI Star Mountain, Inc. ©2003
The • Bargaining • Book

ANSWERS

9. The preparation team is normally larger than the team that will actually do the negotiating. While the preparation team normally includes all members of the negotiating team, it will embrace other segments of the organization necessary to properly prepare. In addition to these practical concerns, involving other segments of the organization will also give you an opportunity to have the team gain acceptance throughout the organization and to implement the contract after negotiations are concluded. Mary should make these arguments to her boss who is questioning the size of the preparation team. *The correct answer is A.*

10. Mary should consider all of these. *The correct answer is D.*

11. Preparing the data necessary to substantiate a proposal is an essential function of the preparation team . In traditional negotiations, the object of a bargaining session is to persuade the other team a proposal has merit. One of the best ways to do this is to convince your counterparts that the proposal is well thought through; that the proposal is feasible; and that the proposal is affordable. Analyzing economic data in this way is time-consuming, but necessary. Also, both parties will want the final product to succeed. A well-researched proposal is more likely to lead to successful implementation.

If the subject is important, the time spent in gathering the necessary data to support it is time well spent. *The correct answer is B.*

QUESTIONS

Bargaining Team Guidelines

The Bargaining Team Should:

• Have 3-5 members

• Be inolved in drafting the proposal

• Reflect institutional concerns

• Have a well-defined purpose for each member

12. Mary Jamison is attempting to determine who will represent the agency in negotiations. She knows that she will be the chief negotiator and will have the assistance of a personnel management specialist but has not made any other decisions concerning the team's structure. Negotiations will not begin for another six months and she is receiving conflicting advice on the number and type of other people that should be involved. What should she do?

FPMI
Star Mountain, Inc.
© 2 0 0 3

A. If possible, push for selection of the team members now to allow them to become knowledgeable about the bargaining process and to establish the agency's objectives.

B. Wait until approximately one month before the start of negotiations to force a decision from management on the other team members.

C.   Prepare the proposal and negotiate the agreement herself with the assistance of one other member of her staff or another employee from within the personnel office.

13. Sam McLean is also attempting to determine who should be on his bargaining team. The views of his membership are controlled by a small group of active members and at least one of these activists would like to unseat him in the union's election of officers that is coming up next year.

He is considering asking a national representative to serve as the chief negotiator but knows that this person would be unable to help in drafting the proposal or training the team members. Which course of action would he best be advised to follow?

A. Rely on the national representative to do most of the work, provide the expertise and select the team shortly before negotiations begin. This will enable Sam to blame a person from outside the local if there is criticism of the agreement or the union team later.

B. Attempt to have his potential opponent serve as the chief negotiator and then attempt to place any blame on him for any faults or criticism of the new agreement.

C. Serve as the chief negotiator himself, rely on the national representative for technical advice and expertise, and try to have his potential opponent serve as a member of the bargaining team.

NOTES

FPMI
Star Mountain, Inc.
© 2 0 0 3

The • Bargaining • Book

ANSWERS

12. It is generally advisable to select the bargaining team at least several months in advance of the negotiations to allow them to become familiar with the existing agreement and to assist in formulating proposals or objectives. This serves two important functions: first, the proposal will be a better one because it will have been developed by a team with broader experience throughout the organization. Second, it will enable the team to gain the credibility that is essential if the final agreement is to be accepted by the organization. In other words, it will not be viewed solely as a product of the personnel office or the product of the chief negotiator. It requires the other portions of the organization to "buy-in" to the agreement and to share the responsibility for the final product and the responsibility for the success or failure in the administration of the agreement. *The correct answer is A.*

13. For the agreement to have any realistic possibility of success, the members of the local must have responsibility for the initial proposal and responsibility for reaching the final agreement. Choices A and B do not provide a firm basis for Sam's team to begin negotiating. These approaches almost guarantee that the union will end up with a contract that no one likes and for which no one will claim responsibility. Relying on a national representative to provide the technical advice and guidance makes sense but attempting to place the blame on a person who is necessarily an "outsider" may serve the short term goals for Sam but will not do him or his local justice in the long run. *The correct answer is C.*

Critical Bargaining Team Roles

- Chief Negotiator
- Labor Relations Expert
- Note-taker
- Personnel Expert
- Establishing Credibility

QUESTIONS

14. In addition to the institutional concerns discussed above, Mary Jamison needs to decide what areas of expertise she should have represented on her team. She is inclined not to include a high level manager on the team because of the time involved in the bargaining process and the limited time available to any senior official. Should she consider having a senior manager on the team?

A. Yes, because it will give the management team credibility with the union and provide the team with a broad knowledge of the agency's activities and objectives that are available only from a member of senior management.

The•Bargaining•Book
FPMI Star Mountain, Inc. ©2003

B. Yes, because the labor relations statute requires a senior management official to be a team member.

C. No, because a senior manager will not devote the time and attention necessary to do a good job.

15. Sam McLean has asked one of the local's officers to take notes during the negotiations. This offended the officer and he told Sam to "hire a good secretary—I won't waste my time." As a result, Sam is inclined to forget about taking notes during the negotiations. What should he do?

A. Forget having a note-taker on the team. The only item of importance is the final agreement anyway.

B. Hire someone with excellent note-taking skills.

C. Use someone knowledgeable about labor relations and who is familiar with the issues to take the notes during the bargaining sessions.

NOTES

FPMI Star Mountain, Inc. © 2003 **The • Bargaining • Book**

ANSWERS

14. Any bargaining team needs to have credibility. Without credibility, the ability of the team to persuade the other side that its arguments and positions are viable will be difficult or impossible. One way to obtain this credibility is to demonstrate that management takes the negotiations seriously by having one or more members of senior management actively participate in the negotiations.

Also, having a member of senior management on the team will provide the team with a broad management perspective normally unavailable to members that are in a lower position within the organization. A member of senior management is much more likely to be more knowledgeable of the philosophy and goals of the activity. Mary's concern about the amount of time available to a member of senior management to spend on the team is well-founded.

Some agencies believe that having a senior manager on the team is beneficial. However, if that person is generally unavailable or does not participate in the bargaining sessions, it is not likely to be useful. Little credibility will be gained and there will not be compensating advantages for the team. In short, having a senior manager on the team is a good idea. However, ensure that he or she will really be on the team and not a figurehead that does not participate in the proceedings.

The actual position occupied by the senior manager is not as important as the items noted. Some agencies may use a senior official as a chief negotiator. Others will give these duties to another person.
Make this decision based upon your analysis of the strengths and weaknesses of the individuals with whom you are dealing. That is likely to be much more successful that trying to impose artificial rules on different situations. *The correct answer is A.*

15. A note-taker is an essential part of any bargaining team. Contrary to the belief expressed by Sam's team member, the position of note-taker requires a broad knowledge of the issues being considered and discussed during the bargaining sessions as well as a knowledge of labor relations concepts and principles.

The notes are useful in two ways. First, the team will need to know what has been discussed; what concessions have been made throughout the bargaining sessions; and what issues remain to be considered. No one person can remember all of these items. Second, the notes are useful to interpreting and applying the contract after it has been signed and implemented. For example, if the parties to the agreement cannot agree what was meant by a contract clause or disagree as to

FPMI Star Mountain, Inc. © 2003

the intent of the bargaining teams when the clause was agreed upon, the notes available will be invaluable.

Keeping good notes during an active bargaining session is not easy. It requires concentration, stamina, and an understanding of what is being discussed at any given time. Sam is wise to consider this in deciding who will fulfill this important function. Sam could also consider discussing with Mary the possibility of having a joint note-taker. This person could prepare one set of notes for approval by both teams, particularly in interest-based bargaining. Using this technique may work well. *The correct answer is C.*

With the increased usage of computers and screen projection programs, some negotiators are utilizing the services of an individual who can enter the initial proposals of both parties for a particular article and maintain the status of each party's counter-proposals. This record is viewed by the negotiators during the negotiation process and printed when the article is finalized as the record for the proceeding. While the bargaining team members will continue to maintain individual notes, an identified note-taker on each team may still be necessary.

QUESTIONS

16. In evaluating candidates for the bargaining team, Mary's boss suggests she consider a person well-known for his temper and dislike of unions. Should she consider this person for the team?

> A. Yes, because he will intimidate the union team and enable management to obtain a better agreement.

An Effective Team Member
• Ability to tolerate conflict and ambiguity
• Patience
• Open-minded and a Good Listener
• Perceptive
• Insists on Integrity at all Times

B. Yes, but he should not be the chief negotiator. She should use him only when necessary to "bluster and bluff" the union team.

C. No, because he is likely to be unpredictable and may cause dissension.

17. Sam wants to select as a team member a person who is highly-thought of by his peers and by management because he gets along well with people and is known as a person who always keeps his word in any dealings he has with others. Is Sam making a mistake putting this person on his team?

A. No, because a person with a favorable reputation will be more persuasive in dealing with the other team.

B. Yes, because the other team will think he is an easy target and they are likely to take advantage of the situation.

C. Yes, because he should attempt to get employees on the team with a reputation for being obstinate and vocal in order to keep the management team from getting away with anything.

NOTES

The•Bargaining•Book

FPMI
Star Mountain, Inc.
© 2003

ANSWERS

16. While the ability to tolerate conflict and ambiguity is an essential attribute for any team member, knowingly staffing the bargaining team with a person who will create tension and conflict is a mistake. A person with this type of personality will create more problems for the management team than for the union. As chief negotiator, Mary will have to play the role of a mediator with her own team members on many occasions. Including a person on the team who does not accept unions and with a temper will make her job much more difficult.

Additionally, an experienced negotiator will work hard to maintain the integrity of the team at all times. While a bad temper and a dislike of unions is not synonymous with a lack of integrity, a lack of respect for the role played by the other team (regardless of whether the other side is the management or the union team) will make it much more difficult to maintain control and to reach an agreement. *Therefore, the correct answer is C.*

17. Sam's decision to include on the team a person with a good reputation is a wise one. The object of any negotiations is to reach agreement. If the other side has a favorable impression of the unions' team members, they will be more receptive to the union's concerns and interests. The object should not be merely to irritate the other side but to decide how to quickly and effectively reach an agreement that satisfies both parties. *The correct answer is A.*

Anticipating Proposals

To anticipate what the other team will propose, it is useful to look for:
- Grievances

- Complaints

- Other Agencies

- Other Unions

18. Mary Jamison asks one of her preparation team members to check union contracts with other agencies that deal with the same parent union. One of her team members asks her why she wants that done since they are dealing with a different local union and different people. Since the national union is not in charge of the negotiations, why would Mary want this information?

A. Many proposals or issues that surface in one agency are likely to be made in another one.

B. It makes all members of the preparation team feel useful by contributing something to the team effort.

C. Since most local unions want their contract to be unique, they are likely to avoid trying to include in their contract the same proposals contained in contracts with other agencies. Therefore, Mary's request for the information will not be very useful to her bargaining team.

19. Sam McLean asks one of his team members to review the responses made by the agency to all grievances filed by the local throughout the life of the existing agreement. Why would this information be useful to the union?

A. The information requested by Sam is not likely to be of any value because the agency can reopen any contract article during the bargaining process.

B. The agency's response to the union's grievances would be useful in anticipating proposals as the responses are likely to show what problems management perceives in the existing agreement and which articles they are likely to try to change during the negotiations.

C. Since management only responds to proposals made by the union and does not make any of its own proposals at the outset of the bargaining process, Sam's request is misplaced.

FPMI
Star Mountain, Inc.
© 2 0 0 3

ANSWERS

18. Local unions often rely on the experience of other locals and their national office when preparing their proposals. Some unions prepare model contract language (i.e., contract proposals that the union considers to be good ones to include in an agreement) that the local union is likely to use. It is often difficult for an agency to know to what extent a local union will rely on these outside sources but the review of other contracts and even proposals from other locals, particularly within the same agency, will often give a bargaining team a preview of what is to be presented. Having this information in advance will assist in preparing its proposals or establishing objectives. *The correct answer is A.*

19. The responses made by an agency to grievances filed by a union or an employee during the life of a contract may provide insight into what changes the management team may seek in the negotiations. Management has the same right to seek changes in the contract by making proposals at the outset of the negotiations as the union does. A well-prepared bargaining team will go through these same preparations whether the team is representing management or the union. *The correct answer is B.*

QUESTIONS

20. Sam McLean wants one location for all items exchanged on each article. He instructs members of the preparation team to prepare an analysis of articles assigned to them and to then distribute this analysis to the other team members. One of the team members tells him he is "wasting his time on this nonsense and to get down to business." What should Sam do now?

The Bargaining Book

A bargaining book is used to:

• Hold essential documents

• Record proposals and counter-proposals

• Provide easy access to information during the bargaining sessions

A. Sam should explain that the analysis of each proposal will be essential to defending the union's position to the agency team and any third parties involved.

B. Sam should tell the dissenting team member not to bother with the analysis if he does not want to do it as it will only be useful if the union has to file a negotiability appeal. (A negotiability appeal determines whether one of the union's proposals is a proper subject for bargaining under the labor relations statute.)

FPMI
Star Mountain, Inc.
© 2003

The • Bargaining • Book

C. He should simply ask the team member to be prepared to argue in favor of his assigned articles when the subject of the article is to be discussed with the management team during the negotiations.

21. One of the team members questions Sam as to why he wants to bother with keeping all proposals and counter-proposals since the only thing that counts is the final product anyway. What would Sam's best response be?

A. Keeping accurate records maintains team discipline and the union's national office will want to see the bargaining book to help other locals around the country.

B. Keeping these records will help the union win if an unfair labor practice is filed against the union team by the agency during the course of the negotiations.

C. Keeping accurate records will be invaluable in determining the intent of the union's proposal in the administration of the agreement; it will assist the union in convincing a third party why its position is the most convincing if an impasse is reached; and it will enable the union to keep track of where it stands during the negotiations.

NOTES

The • Bargaining • Book

FPMI
Star Mountain, Inc.
© 2003

ANSWERS

20. The bargaining book will be important both during the negotiations and after the new agreement is signed. It is valuable during the negotiations as it will help the team keep track of the progress of negotiations on each article. It also provides a convenient spot to put all documents relating to a particular article so these documents can easily be found and referenced during the actual negotiating process. A negotiator that cannot find his notes and reference points during the negotiations has placed himself at a disadvantage during the bargaining. The bargaining book will also serve a useful purpose in arguing on a negotiability appeal if it becomes necessary to file one. (Negotiability will be discussed in more detail in the next chapter.) If an unfair labor practice is filed, the bargaining book will be a useful defense in demonstrating the union's good faith attempts to reach agreement.

These notes will also prove to be invaluable if the parties later disagree over the meaning of the negotiated agreement. Such disagreements are normally resolved through a process that results in a mutual interpretation of the article in question. However, if the parties cannot arrive at a mutual interpretation, the disagreement may result in grievance arbitration. In an arbitration process, the notes of the negotiators are extremely important since the arbitrator must attempt to interpret the actual intent of the parties when the article was negotiated.

For these reasons, Sam should strive to maintain team discipline and have each member do his part to maintain the bargaining book. *The correct answer is A.*

21. It is important to any bargaining team to maintain records of all proposals and counter-proposals. It is particularly useful in attempting to determine the intent of contract language during the administration of the agreement. It also helps the team keep track of its position on each article during the negotiations. *The correct answer is C.*

Rules·of·the·Bargaining·Process

Chapter 3

FPMI
Star Mountain, Inc.

Rules of the Bargaining Process

Rules are not usually much fun and are often intended to constrain actions of the participants. But, for better or worse, there are certain rules that must be followed by a federal sector negotiator. If you do not know the rules, learning them solely through experience will be a painful, personal experience and turn a process that is normally slow into one that is even slower.

Learn the rules before starting negotiations. Not knowing them may lead to extensive litigation and acrimony both within your team and with the opposing team. This lack of knowledge may also embarrass you and the institution you are representing. It can affect the credibility of your agency or your union. This chapter will teach you the general rules within which you must work to effectively bargain in the federal sector.

Keep in mind that the labor relations field is dynamic and, therefore, constantly changing. New decisions and policies are frequently issued by the Federal Labor Relations Authority, the courts, or others with authority to influence the process. Therefore, it would be wise to consult with a labor relations expert whenever deciding whether a proposal is negotiable. The examples given in this chapter, particularly in the negotiability arena, are correct as of the time *The Bargaining Book* was updated but existing decisions are always subject to change as new case decisions are issued.

After reading this chapter, you will know:

- What ground rules are and how they impact federal labor negotiations.

- The meaning of the phrase "prohibited subjects of bargaining" and how this will impact your bargaining sessions.

- The meaning of the phrase "permissive subjects of bargaining" and how this will impact your bargaining sessions.

- The meaning of the phrase "mandatory subjects of bargaining" and how this will impact your bargaining sessions.

- How negotiability questions are resolved.

- When an employee is entitled to official time to negotiate an agreement.

- The required contents of a negotiated grievance procedure.

© 2003

• Limitations on the coverage of a negotiated grievance procedure.

• The purpose of arbitration.

• How an arbitrator is selected.

QUESTIONS

22. In drafting ground rules to submit to the agency, Sam wants to propose that the negotiations be conducted in a meeting room away from the worksite and that the agency and the union will split any costs incurred. Can he propose this?

Ground Rules

• Not required by law or regulation

• Subject to negotiation

• Cover length and frequency of negotiations, number of team members, use of time by union negotiators, etc.

A. No, the labor relations statute requires that negotiations be held on the premises of the federal government.

B. He can propose that the negotiations be held at a neutral site but the Comptroller General has ruled that an agency cannot pay for any of these expenses. Therefore, the union will have to pay any costs associated with securing a room at a neutral site.

C. Yes, he can propose this. The agency does not have to agree but the issue is subject to negotiation between the two parties.

23. After writing his proposal on ground rules, Sam informs the agency that he would like to negotiate on this subject. After reviewing the proposal, Mary Jamison tells him that ground rules are unnecessary and a waste of time. Furthermore, she added, the agency does not intend to bother with them in these negotiations. What options does Sam have?

A. Since both sides are obligated to negotiate on ground rules he could properly tell Mary that he will insist on negotiating them and will enforce his right through the unfair labor practice procedures of the labor relations statute if necessary.

B. Mary can properly refuse to negotiate on ground rules. Therefore, Sam will have to accept her decision and prepare his team as best he can.

C. As ground rules are uncommon in the federal sector, he should accept her decision and proceed to negotiate, as most parties do, by negotiating the procedures with the agency on an "as needed" basis.

ANSWERS

22. The site for the negotiations to be held is a proper subject of bargaining. While it is not always done in the federal sector because of the costs associated with obtaining a site away from the worksite or because it is viewed as being unnecessary by the parties to the negotiations, Sam has a right to pursue the issue through the bargaining procedures. An agency is not precluded from paying for such an arrangement although, as in all issues open to negotiation, it is not obligated to agree to such an arrangement either. *The correct answer is C.*

23. The ground rules to be used during negotiations, while not required by law, are a proper subject of bargaining. Therefore, each side has an obligation to make a good faith effort to try to reach agreement on ground rules. If the agency persists in refusing to negotiate on them, Sam could enforce his right to negotiate on ground rules through the unfair labor practice mechanism outlined in the labor relations statute. *The correct answer is A.*

Bargaining Categories

Bargaining subjects are in one of these categories:

• Mandatory

• Permissive

• Prohibited

QUESTIONS

24. In the union's proposal, an article was included that would require the agency to purchase a specific brand of computers for all new terminals installed for bargaining unit employees. The bargaining teams have negotiated on the proposal for several sessions but have failed to reach an agreement. Mary Jamison tells the union that the agency will not bargain on the topic any further because it is a "permissive" subject. Sam acknowledges it is permissive but he still believes the agency has an obligation to bargain on it. Is Sam right?

A. Yes. Permissive topics of bargaining are now open to negotiation between agencies and unions.

B. No. If a topic of bargaining is permissive, an agency may decline to negotiate on it any time prior to reaching agreement.

C. No. It is an unfair labor practice for the union to try and negotiate on the technology used by an agency to perform its work.

The•Bargaining•Book

© 2 0 0 3

25. Mary Jamison proposes that the union will not represent any employee in a grievance unless the employee has been a dues paying member of the union for at least one year.

Sam agrees to the proposal but he is then advised by his national representative that the agreement violates the law and is, in effect, a prohibited subject of bargaining. Mary tells the union team that since an agreement was reached, the union is now obligated to live up to it. Is Mary right?

A. Yes. Once an agreement is reached, the agreement cannot be abrogated even if it is a prohibited subject of bargaining.

B. No, because an agreement that concerns a prohibited subject of bargaining is not legal and cannot be enforced.

C. Yes, once an agreement is reached the subject becomes a mandatory topic of bargaining rather than a prohibited subject of bargaining.

NOTES

FPMI Star Mountain, Inc. © 2003

The • Bargaining • Book

ANSWERS

24. A permissive topic of bargaining is one on which an agency or a union can negotiate or not negotiate on as it sees fit—at least as far as the labor relations statute is concerned. During the time EO 12871 was effective, a great deal of litigation occurred on this issue. The final result is that the Statute took precedence over the EO and agencies retained the right to determine whether they would bargain over permissive subjects. *The correct answer is B.*

25. As discussed earlier in *The Bargaining Book*, a prohibited subject of bargaining is one which is prohibited by the labor relations statute. One right all employees in a unit have is to form, join or assist a union or to refrain from doing so. The union has an obligation to provide the same representation to employees regardless of whether they have elected to join the union.

The agreement reached by Sam and Mary to restrict the right of an employee to union representation until he or she has been a member of the union for at least one year violates the statute. It is a prohibited subject of bargaining. Any agreement reached on a prohibited subject is not enforceable. *The correct answer is B.*

Prohibited Topics

Prohibited topics are usually called management rights. These are not negotiable. These rights include:

• Determining mission, budget and organization

• Determining numbers of employees

• Taking personnel actions and assigning work

• Contracting out work

• Making selections for positions or promotions

• Taking action during emergencies

QUESTIONS

26. Sam proposes to the management team that "all selections for positions within the bargaining unit will be made from employees currently employed within the unit as long as there is at least one employee qualified to fill the position." Mary tells Sam that this is a prohibited subject of bargaining. Is she right?

A. No, because the proposal does not restrict the right of the agency to fill a position with a qualified employee.

B. No, because the agency still has the right to determine whether the employee is qualified.

C. Yes, because the agency has the right to make personnel selections from any appropriate source and this proposal would restrict that right.

The • Bargaining • Book

FPMI
Star Mountain, Inc.
© 2003

27. The union proposes that the agency establish a day care center for children of employees who work in the bargaining unit. Mary tells the union team that the proposal affects the agency's budget as it would cost a considerable sum of money to establish such a center. As it affects the budget, she concludes, it is a prohibited subject of bargaining and the agency will not negotiate on this topic. Is she right?

A. No, because the effect of a day care center on the agency's budget is not direct. The fact that the agency may encounter some expenses for instituting a day care center does not make it non-negotiable.

B. Yes. Since the agency will encounter some expenses for establishing a day care center, the union's proposal effectively determines how the agency's money will be spent and it is therefore a prohibited subject of bargaining.

C. Yes, the subject is a prohibited subject of bargaining unless the union modifies its proposal to agree to pay for any and all expenses associated with establishing a day care center at the agency.

28. The union makes the following proposal: "Prior to awarding a contract to a company to perform work currently done by bargaining unit employees, the union will be given at least 30 days advance notice and sufficient time to bargain on the impact of the decision." Mary tells Sam that this proposal interferes with the agency's right guaranteed by the labor relations statute to contract-out work. Is Mary correct?

A. No, because the union proposal only concerns the impact of the management decision to contract the work. It does not concern the decision itself.

B. Yes, because management has the right to make decisions on contracting work to the private sector.

C. Yes, because the union's proposal may delay management's implementation of the decision to contract with a private company to do the work.

FPMI
Star Mountain, Inc.
© 2 0 0 3
The • Bargaining • Book

ANSWERS

26. A union proposal that requires management to select an employee from the bargaining unit for a position is a prohibited subject of bargaining. While the union's proposal appears to have left to the agency the decision as to which employees are qualified, an agency may still wish to select a person from outside the unit. The union's proposal would preclude this and the proposal therefore is contrary to the requirements of the labor relations statute. *The correct answer is C.*

Keep in mind that it may be possible to avoid a negotiability dispute by focusing on the concerns of each party rather than negotiability. For example, it may be possible to satisfy the interests of both parties with an agreement to first consider unit employees for a vacancy before making a final selection.

In other words, it is usually a good idea to concentrate on resolving the dispute rather than fighting over specific words.

27. Establishing a day care center is a proper subject of bargaining. While establishing a day care center may impact an agency's budget, the impact is considered by the Federal Labor Relations Authority to be indirect or secondary. The agency is therefore obligated to bargain with the union to the extent that it has discretion to act in establishing such a center. The agency could take the position that there are insufficient funds and refuse to agree to establishing a day care center for that reason. Keep in mind, however, that this is an argument that can be used to persuade the union or a third party but it does not negate the obligation to bargain on the subject. *The correct answer is A.*

28. The union's proposal concerns a negotiable procedure. Event though the proposal would delay the implementation of the management decision if it was included in a collective bargaining agreement, the FLRA weighs whether the proposal "excessively interferes" with the implementation of the management right. Current decisions of the FLRA have interpreted that a proposal of this type does not prevent the agency from "acting at all" but rather provides the bargaining unit with some procedures that could mitigate the affect of a management decision made under Section 7106 (a)(1)(A) of the statute. Management decisions made under that section of the statute are subject to negotiations with the Union on how the decision will be implemented and the impact that decision will have on the bargaining unit employees. Based on existing decisions of the FLRA, this proposal would not "excessively interfere" with the management right and is a proper subject of bargaining. *The correct answer is A.*

FPMI
Star Mountain, Inc.
© 2 0 0 3

29. Sam McLean believes that the agency has plans to install a new computer system that will result in reducing the number of clerical employees employed by the agency. As the union represents these clerical employees, it is an issue that is of major importance to the union in contract negotiations. The union team proposes that no new computers will be installed by the agency if any employees will lose their jobs. Is the management team obligated to negotiate on the union's proposal?

> # Permissive Topics
>
> On permissive topics, an agency may negotiate on the topic if it wishes — it is not required by law to negotiate on it. Permissive topics are:
>
> • Numbers, types, and grades of positions
>
> • Positions assigned to an organization
>
> • Technology, methods, or means of performing work

A. Yes, because the subject has a direct impact on the job security of the bargaining unit.

B. Yes, because the proposal concerns a condition of employment within the control of the agency.

C. No, because the proposal concerns the technology of performing work of the unit.

30. Sam has received a number of inquiries from union members concerning the grades of employees assigned to the agency's offices in Washington, D.C., and San Francisco, California. Employees in those offices believe that they should be a higher grade than employees in other locations because of the cost of living and because of the higher number of customers they service. As a result of these complaints, Sam proposes that the agency will assign work normally performed by GS-12's to the San Francisco and Washington offices and that the employees in those offices will be paid at the GS-12 level. Is the union entitled to negotiate this issue?

A. No, because it concerns the right of the agency to assign work and classification issues that are normally outside the obligation to bargain.

B. Yes, because cost of living expenses are a condition of employment.

C. Yes, because the proposal gives the agency flexibility in what work will be performed and only requires that work already classified at a GS-12 level will be performed in San Francisco and Washington.

FPMI
Star Mountain, Inc.
© 2 0 0 3
The • Bargaining • Book

ANSWERS

29. The union's proposal concerns the use of technology — a permissive topic of bargaining. The end result of this situation is similar to that described in question 28 but this situation is a permissive subject of bargaining. The agency is still obligated to bargain on the impact and implementation of such a decision but not on the decision itself. The parties should focus their efforts on the <u>interests</u> of both sides to look for a solution. For example, it may be possible to reassign or retrain employees to use the new technology or use existing employee skills elsewhere in the agency but to go ahead with plans for the new computer system with this person. *The correct answer is A.*

30. An agency has the statutory right to decide where specific work will be performed and it is likely that this proposal would be found to be a topic that is outside the obligation to bargain. *The correct answer is A.*

QUESTIONS

Mandatory Topics

Mandatory topics of bargaining are:

• Conditions of employment for unit employees

• Consistent with law and government-wide regulations

• Impact and implementation of management rights

31. The union team proposes an article prohibiting the assignment of employees to a different location without prior negotiation with the union on the impact of this decision. Should the agency negotiate on this topic?

A. Yes. The union is entitled to negotiate on the impact of the management decision to assign work and direct employees.

B. No. The assignment of employees is a prohibited subject of bargaining rather than a mandatory one.

C. Yes, it is a mandatory subject because it concerns a condition of employment.

32. The union team makes the following proposal: "The agency agrees to pay a minimum of 90% of the cost of an employee's health insurance premium as long as the employee is participating in a government-sponsored health insurance plan." Is this negotiable?

A. No, because health insurance is not a condition of employment.

B. Yes, because health insurance is a condition of employment.

C. No, because the amount of the government's contribution to a health insurance program is not within the discretion of the agency.

The•Bargaining•Book

ANSWERS

31. Management has the right to direct employees and to assign work. Therefore, the decision on whether to make an assignment of an employee or a group of employees to a particular location is a reserved management right. In this case, Sam has recognized that management has this right. However, his proposal would allow the union to negotiate on the impact of the management decision; it would not require negotiation of the actual decision to reassign employees. The assignment of employees may affect conditions of employment such as promotion potential and the nature of an employee's assignments.

The reasons set forth in the answer to question 28 are applicable here. This type bargaining is commonly referenced as Impact and Implementation or I&I bargaining. In this case, while management has the right to assign employees, the union is entitled to negotiate on the implementation of that management decision. *The correct answer is A.*

32. The subject of health insurance premiums would normally appear to fall under the definition of a "condition of employment" contained in the labor relations statute. However, the amount of the government's contribution to the payment of health insurance is not a subject over which the agency has any control as it is controlled by law or government-wide regulation. *The correct answer is C.*

QUESTIONS

33. The union team proposes that the agency allow all employees to choose whether to receive their paychecks at work, at home, or electronically deposited to a bank. Mary tells Sam the proposal is not a proper subject of bargaining because it is contrary to a government-wide rule or regulation. What can Sam do now?

Negotiability Determinations

Questions on negotiability are:

• Resolved by the Federal labor Relations Authority

• Filed only by a union

A. He must accept the agency's decision.

B. He can appeal the agency's determination of non-negotiability to the Federal Labor Relations Authority.

C. He must ask the agency to file an appeal.

Star Mountain, Inc.
© 2003

34. Mary proposes that the union designate the chief steward to handle all formal grievances and that the local union president be designated to handle grievances that proceed to arbitration. Sam tells her that as far as he is concerned, the agency's proposal is not negotiable because it affects the ability of the union to designate its own representatives. What options does Mary have to contest the union's declaration of non-negotiability?

A. She must accept the union's decision.

B. She can file a negotiability appeal with the Federal Labor Relations Authority.

C. She can file an unfair labor practice against the union for bargaining in bad faith.

NOTES

FPMI
Star Mountain, Inc.
© 2 0 0 3

ANSWERS

33. The union does not have to accept the agency's decision on negotiability. Obviously, Sam can accept it if he wishes. The effect of a decision to accept the agency's determination on the negotiability question would be that the issue will be outside the scope of bargaining because the union has not challenged it.

If the union wants to contest the agency's determination, it may file a negotiability appeal with the FLRA. The union must first request a written determination by the agency and the union's appeal must be filed within 15 days after the agency statement of non-negotiability is served on the union. (Sam would, incidentally, win his appeal as the FLRA has determined that this issue concerns a condition of employment and is therefore a mandatory subject of bargaining.) *Therefore, the correct answer is B.*

34. An agency cannot file a negotiability appeal with the FLRA because, under the FLRA's regulations, an agency is not entitled to use this procedure. If Mary wishes to contest the union's decision that the proposal is not negotiable, she would have to file an unfair labor practice against the union alleging that the union is not bargaining in good faith because it has refused to negotiate on a mandatory subject of bargaining. (She would, incidentally, lose the case because the FLRA has determined that a union or an agency has the right to select its own representatives.) *Therefore, the correct answer is C.*

Official Time

An employee receives official time (paid time) when:

- The employee is representing the union

- The employee would normally be on duty

- The number of union representatives does not exceed the number of management representatives

35. Mary Jamison has refused the union's request to give official time to five union team members because the agency will have only four team members. Sam argues that each member is essential because each one is a subject matter expert on an issue that will surface during the negotiations. Mary still refused to grant the time to the extra negotiator proposed by the union. Is Mary's position justified?

A. No, because it is customary to have at least five members on each negotiating team and the agency's position is not reasonable.

B. Yes, because the number of union negotiators on official time cannot exceed the number of management negotiators.

C. No, because the agency is attempting to direct the internal affairs of the union.

36. Sam McLean has included on his team an employee of the agency who works for a small part of the organization that is outside the bargaining unit represented by the union. Is this person entitled to receive official time?

A. Yes, because he is a federal employee and is representing the local union.

B. Yes, as long as he would normally be in a duty status.

C. No, because he is not an employee of the bargaining unit.

NOTES

The • Bargaining • Book

FPMI
Star Mountain, Inc.
© 2 0 0 3

ANSWERS

35. The union is only entitled to the same number of union negotiators on official time that the agency has. The labor relations statute does not require that any particular number of negotiators be designated. While the union's request for five negotiators is not unreasonable or illegal, there is no requirement that the agency comply with it. The union could negotiate with the agency to have a larger number than the agency has designated but the agency does not have to agree with Sam's proposal. *The correct answer is B.*

36. The only employees entitled to receive official time to engage in contract negotiations are those in the bargaining unit represented by the union. If an employee of the agency is outside the bargaining unit, he is not entitled to receive official time. *Therefore, the correct answer is C.*

QUESTIONS

37. In the agency's proposal for a grievance procedure, the agency has included a section giving employees the right to use any representative he or she wishes to use when pursuing a grievance. Sam objects and claims that the agency's proposal violates the law. Is he correct?

Grievance Procedure

All agreements must have a grievance procedure. Each grievance procedure:

• Must include an arbitration provision

• Must be fair and simple

• Is normally the only procedure available

• Prohibits outside representation of employees

    A. Yes. Employees are precluded from using their own representative when using the negotiated grievance procedure.

B. No. Employees are entitled to have a representative of their own choosing when pursuing a grievance.

C. No. As long as the grievance has not gone to arbitration the employee can select his or her own representative.

38. The union team is concerned about the possible workload that will result from the new grievance procedure. To prevent the local from being overwhelmed, Sam proposes that employees will have a choice of using the agency grievance procedure (that does not include arbitration) or the negotiated grievance procedure (which does end in arbitration).

The agency team is inclined to accept the proposal but Mary is concerned that it is not proper to include such a provision. Is she right to be concerned?

A. No, as long as employees have a choice, there is no violation of the statute.

B. No, as long as the union agrees, because use of the grievance procedure is subject to negotiation between the agency and the union.

C. Yes. Employees are normally required to use the negotiated grievance procedure.

NOTES

FPMI Star Mountain, Inc. ©2003

ANSWERS

37. An employee is restricted when using the grievance procedure to self-representation or union representation. Since this is a requirement of law, management and the union cannot negotiate a provision that is contrary to the legal requirements imposed by the statute. However, the FLRA has acknowledged that the Union may approve a non-union representative for the employee, but that is totally at the discretion of the Union. This situation has normally occurred where the employee is being disciplined and wants to utilize the services of an attorney. It would be an Unfair Labor Practice for management to recognize a non-union representative without Union approval. *The correct answer is A.*

38. Mary is right to be concerned. Employees must use the negotiated grievance procedure in most cases.

The only exceptions are grievances concerning equal employment opportunity (EEO) complaints, actions based on unacceptable performance and adverse actions. Therefore, the employees cannot properly be given the option of using the agency grievance procedure in lieu of the negotiated grievance procedure even if the agency and the union are in agreement. *The correct answer is C.*

QUESTIONS

39. Mary Jamison proposes that the scope of the grievance procedure be limited so it would exclude an employee from grieving adverse actions. Sam tells her that the scope of the procedure is determined by statute and that management and the union are not free to negotiate on the scope of the procedure. Who is right?

    A. Sam is right. The scope of the procedure is determined by statute and the only limitations are those listed above.

Grievance Procedure Limitations

Topics that cannot be grieved include:

- Hatch Act violations

- Retirement, life insurance, or health insurance problems

- Suspension or removal for national security

- Any examination, certification, or appointment

- Classification of a position not resulting in reduction in grade or pay

    B. Neither Sam nor Mary is right. Mary is right that the scope of the procedure is negotiable but the parties cannot exclude adverse actions from the procedure as she has done in her proposal. Sam is incorrect in that the scope of the procedure is otherwise negotiable.

C. Mary is right. The scope of the procedure is negotiable as long as it does not include the limitations listed above.

40. Sam's team wants to ensure that any employee who is reclassified has a chance to challenge that classification decision through the grievance procedure. Can this be done?

A. No, because the proposal includes the grieving of classification decisions that do not result in the reduction in grade or pay of an employee.

B. Yes, because it includes the grieving of classification decisions that result in the reduction in grade or pay of an employee.

C. Yes, because the scope of the grievance procedure is negotiable.

NOTES

The•Bargaining•Book

FPMI
Star Mountain, Inc.
© 2003

ANSWERS

39. The scope of the grievance procedure is negotiable to the extent that it cannot include any of the restricted subjects.

Also, as you learned in the previous section, the parties cannot formulate a procedure that takes away the right of the employee to use the statutory procedure to grieve an EEO complaint, an action based on unacceptable performance or an adverse action. In those three cases, management and the union can negotiate a procedure that gives the employee the right to use either the negotiated procedure or the statutory procedure but under no circumstances can an employee be denied the right to use the complaint procedure provided by law. *The correct answer is C.*

40. While the scope of the grievance procedure is negotiable, it cannot include any subjects that the labor relations statute prohibits from being included in the procedure.

A procedure that allows an employee to grieve a classification decision when the decision does not result in the loss of grade or pay of that employee violates the restrictions imposed by the labor relations statute. Note that the parties can agree, however, to include under the coverage of the procedure the grieving of a classification decision that does result in the loss of grade or pay of an employee. In fact, such a classification decision would automatically be included under the grievance procedure unless the procedure states otherwise. This is because the grievance procedure automatically covers all permissible subjects unless management and the union specifically exclude a subject in their agreement. *The correct answer is A.*

QUESTIONS

41. The management team proposes that an arbitration decision in an adverse action case will not be binding on the agency but will provide a basis for the agency to reconsider its decision to take adverse action against an employee. Is this a proper proposal?

A. Yes, as long as the union will agree to it.

B. No, the arbitration process cannot be advisory.

C. No, it is not proper unless the employee agrees to submit a case to advisory arbitration rather than binding arbitration.

Arbitration

A collective bargaining agreement must contain an arbitration procedure. This procedure:

• Provides for outside review of a dispute

• Is invoked only by the agency or the union

• Provides a decision subject to limited appeal

42. Sam McLean has encountered opposition from one of his team members who wants to include a contract clause allowing an employee to go to arbitration even if the union does not think the employee has a good case. Sam believes that the union must retain control over the ability to invoke arbitration. Should he go along with his other team member?

A. He should not go along with his team member because the statute requires that arbitration can only be invoked by management or the union.

B. He should go along with his team member because the law requires that an employee retain the right to personally invoke the arbitration clause of the contract.

C. The issue is a proper subject of bargaining between management and the union so Sam should see what the other team members want to do.

NOTES

FPMI
Star Mountain, Inc.
© 2 0 0 3

ANSWERS

41. A number of years ago, the federal labor relations program did not require binding arbitration and advisory arbitration clauses were fairly common. When the labor relations statute was passed in 1978, Congress enacted a requirement that federal contracts contain a provision for binding arbitration. Management and the union cannot properly negotiate an advisory arbitration clause. *The correct answer is B.*

42. Management and the union must retain control over the arbitration procedure. While this certainly restricts the individual rights of employees, arbitration is a procedure that management and a union have jointly agreed upon. Both parties should restrict its use to cases that the moving party believes are significant enough to justify the time and expense. *The correct answer is A.*

The Arbitrator

An arbitrator is:

• Selected under the terms of the agreement

• Paid in accordance with the agreement

• Responsible for interpreting coverage of the grievance procedure if there is a dispute

• Required to comply with law and regulation when making decisions

QUESTIONS

43. Mary proposes that the arbitration clause to be included in the new agreement not cover any situation in which the agency decides that the grievance in question is outside the scope of the procedure. Should Sam consider this proposal?

A. Yes, because the scope of the grievance procedure is negotiable.

B. Yes, because the agency retains the right under the statute to determine whether a subject is covered by the grievance procedure.

C. No, because the arbitrator selected by the agency and the union has the authority to decide whether a subject is covered by the grievance procedure.

44. The union proposes that the agency pay all arbitration expenses. Mary tells Sam that a provision requiring an agency or a union to pay all expenses is not proper under the labor relations statute and that the expenses have to be split equally. Is she right?

A. No, the arbitrator decides who should pay the expenses on a case by case basis.

B. No, the issue of who pays for arbitration is negotiable and no one method of payment is required.

C. Yes, she is right because the law requires that management and the union split all of the arbitrator's fees and expenses equally.

NOTES

FPMI Star Mountain, Inc. © 2003

ANSWERS

43. Under the labor relations statute, the arbitrator must decide whether a particular grievance is covered by the procedure. For example, if an employee files a grievance contesting his removal and the union invokes the arbitration provisions of the labor contract, the arbitrator must decide whether the employee can use the grievance procedure or whether he must use the statutory appeal procedure if the agency alleges that the appeal is excluded from the grievance procedure.

The agency can state its position and attempt to convince the arbitrator that a grievance is not covered if it wishes to do so but the alternate method of resolving such an issue as proposed by management is not negotiable. Sam should not consider the proposal. *The correct answer is C.*

44. It is customary that management and the union will split the arbitrator's fees and expenses equally. This is not required, however, and if the parties wish to agree to an alternate procedure they are free to do so.

For example, a limited number of federal sector agreements provide that the loser of an arbitration case will pay all the expenses associated with the case. While this is not common and may not be a good idea since it is frequently hard to know which side won and which side lost a case, it is a proper subject of bargaining. In these cases the arbitrator is generally empowered to determine how his fees will be paid.

Therefore, Mary is not correct because the law does not require that the parties split all costs. The agency does not have to agree to pay all arbitration costs and in most cases would not agree to such a provision, but it is a proper proposal for the union to make. *The correct answer is B.*

Unfair Labor Practices

Unfair Labor Practices (ULP's):

• Can be filed by management or a union

• Can be filed by an employee against management or a union

• Must allege a violation of the labor relations statute

• May be filed at any time within six months after an event

• Are filed with a Regional Director of the FLRA

QUESTIONS

45. In a meeting between Sam and Mary, Sam informs her that he has selected five people for the union's bargaining team. Mary tells him that the agency will only have four people on its team. She adds that the fifth member of the union team will have to take annual leave or be on leave without pay (LWOP) during the negotiations. He then tells Mary he is going to file an unfair labor practice charge if the agency implements this decision. Can Sam do this?

A. No, because ULP charges filed during negotiations will be dismissed by the FLRA.

B. No, because the charge would have to be filed by the employee who does not receive official time. The union cannot file a ULP in this situation.

C. Yes, he can file a ULP charge with the FLRA as he has threatened.

46. The union team has proposed a grievance procedure that would require separate decisions by two different levels of management before the union could invoke arbitration. The agency team has proposed a system with three decision-making levels. Because agreement has not been reached, Mary tells the union team that if they continue to insist on having only two levels, the agency will not agree to have any grievance procedure in the contract. Sam tells her that refusing to include a grievance procedure is an unfair labor practice. Is Sam right?

A. Yes, because the statute requires that each agreement negotiated in the federal sector include a negotiated grievance procedure.

B. No, because the decision on whether to include a grievance procedure is subject to negotiation between the parties.

C. Yes, because once an agency has proposed to include a grievance procedure in the agreement, it is an unfair labor practice to insist that there not be any article on this subject in the contract.

FPMI
Star Mountain, Inc.
© 2 0 0 3

ANSWERS

45. Sam may file a ULP charge. The filing of charges during bargaining is common as each side may attempt to assume a dominant role in the early stages of the negotiations. This charge requires an interpretation of the labor relations statute (i.e., whether the union is entitled to have five team members on official time.). While the employee could file the charge, it is more common for the charge to be filed by the union and the FLRA will accept such a charge. *The correct answer is C as the union could file a ULP charge as Sam has threatened.*

Incidentally, this issue has been the subject of several ULP's. The labor relations statute states that "the number of employees for whom official time is authorized...shall not exceed the number of individuals designated as representing the agency...." In interpreting the statute, however, the FLRA has held that a union may negotiate with the agency on whether it may have a greater number of team members on official time than management. If the agency refuses to negotiate on such a proposal, it is committing a ULP.

46. The labor relations statute requires that all collective bargaining agreements contain a negotiated grievance procedure.

The question that will be considered by the FLRA Regional Director in resolving a case like this is whether the party that has been charged with an unfair labor practice has violated the statute in some way. A third party, such as the FLRA, will be hesitant to become involved in the substance of the negotiations. However, if one party has taken a position that is contrary to the requirements of the law, then the regional director will conclude that there is a basis for issuing a complaint and, in the absence of a settlement, there will be a hearing before an administrative law judge.

Sam's allegation of an unfair labor practice would be correct in this situation since a refusal to include a negotiated grievance procedure would violate the labor regulations statute. *Therefore, the correct answer is A.*

Cooperative•Labor-Management•Relationships

Chapter 4

FPMI
Star Mountain, Inc.

The • Bargaining • Book

Cooperative Labor-Management Relationships

Labor management relations has traditionally been an adversarial process in which the parties, union and management, have competed to see which party can prevail on issues of importance to them. However, in some situations, enlightened parties have found that working together in a cooperative relationship has furthered the goals of both sides, i.e., to provide continuity of employment for the bargaining unit efficiently and effectively. The Federal Service Labor Management Relations Statute provides for such a relationship.

When President Clinton implemented Executive Order 12871 in 1993, he was only reiterating provisions that management could already practice under the Statute. The primary emphasis of the EO, interest based bargaining, negotiation of permissible topics, establishment of Partnership Councils, and working in a more cooperative atmosphere, were not proscribed by the Statute. The problems with implementation far outweighed the wording of the EO. There was disagreement between many of the political appointees and many career employees over the procedures to be implemented and whether the EO would take precedence over the Statute. The career employees were reticent to negotiate permissive topics into the negotiated agreements and this gave rise to numerous unfair labor practice charges. These charges resulted in decisions in which the Federal Labor Relations Authority finally determined that an Executive Order could not take precedence over a Statute.

President Bush subsequently rescinded EO 12871 and abolished the National Partnership Council. However, the other provisions of the Statute, which were embodied with the EO, can continue, although many agencies have changed the name of partnership councils to something more politically sensitive.

After completing this chapter, you should be aware of:

- The rights of the parties concerning negotiation of permissive topics in cooperative arrangements.

- How to use Memoranda of Agreement or Memoranda of Understanding in cooperative arrangements.

- Effective use of cooperative arrangements to resolve day-to-day problems.

© 2003

• The effect cooperative relationships can have on negotiations.

• Some of the changes in conduct of the parties necessary to effectively establish a cooperative labor-management relationship.

QUESTIONS

47. The parties have agreed to develop a cooperative labor management process that will be more harmonious and less litigious. Accordingly, Sam presents a new proposal to Mary that states the parties will negotiate on permissive subjects and incorporate the results of those negotiations as an addendum to the agreement they are currently negotiating. Mary refuses to accede to this position and explains that management wants a more cooperative relationship but is not willing to include any permissive topics in the agreement. How should the parties proceed?

Goals of Cooperative Labor-Management Arrangements

• Resolve issues between the parties in a more harmonious manner

• Eliminate the use of the Unfair Labor Practice procedure through more effective dialog between parties.

• Involve the union in situations affecting the bargaining unit before management makes their final decision

• Develop more trust between management and union representatives

A. Forget having a cooperative relationship at this point and proceed with an adversarial process.

B. Agree to deal with permissive issues in a memorandum of agreement that is not part of the negotiated agreement but deals with how the parties will cooperate to resolve labor management issues.

C. The Union should grieve the refusal of management to include these permissive topics in the agreement since an arbitrator might give a decision different than the FLRA.

48. Sam discovers that management is planning to make some organizational changes during negotiations that might have an adverse effect on two employees. Today, he raises the issue at the start of negotiations and wants to immediately negotiate on these changes. Mary states that she is unaware of the changes Sam has referenced and is not prepared to negotiate on them. If the parties want to build a cooperative relationship, they should do which of the following?

A. Stop scheduled negotiations and investigate this situation to immediately resolve the issue.

B. Mary should assure Sam that the changes will not be taking effect today and that she will investigate the situation and provide appropriate notification to the Union before any changes occur.

C. Contact the manager making the changes and ask that manager to come to negotiations to present the changes that are planned.

49. At lunch today, Mary calls the manager referenced in the question above. He confirms that the changes are planned, have been announced to the staff, and are scheduled to be implemented tomorrow. At the same time, Sam is contacted by the two affected employees and presented with the same information. When negotiations resume after lunch, Mary and Sam should do which of the following if they want to build a cooperative relationship?

A. Sam should present Mary with a copy of an Unfair Labor Practice Charge he is filing with the FLRA.

B. Mary should relate what she found out in her phone call and tell the Union she cannot do anything about the situation.

C. Mary should relate what she found out and tell Sam that the changes will not occur tomorrow because she has informed the manager that his actions could constitute an Unfair Labor Practice for bypassing the Union.

50. Sam proposes a new article for consideration of the parties that incorporates wording in the agreement concerning a cooperative labor management relationship. His wording in the proposal commits the parties to obtain training on cooperative labor management relationships as well as describing goals for the relationship and prescribing that a joint committee will be responsible for this relationship. Mary's response to this proposal should be:

A. The creation of committees involves assignment of work and is not negotiable because it is a reserved management right to assign work.

FPMI
Star Mountain, Inc.
© 2 0 0 3

B. Cooperative labor management relationships should not be memorialized in the negotiated agreement but should be contained in a Memorandum of Understanding.

C. The wording proposed is negotiable and the parties should be careful not to put anything in the negotiated agreement that they may wish to change later in the relationship.

NOTES

ANSWERS

47. The decisions on questions about incorporating permissive topics in negotiated agreements resulted in a determination that management retains the right to determine if they will negotiate on these topics. Accordingly, most organizations that have cooperative relationships between labor and management have a Memorandum of Agreement or Memorandum of Understanding that spells out how the parties will function. If the parties decide to change the MOA or MOU, they are free to do so without involving agency headquarters, which must be involved in changing a negotiated agreement. Any other topics, which are dealt with through the cooperative relationship, could be incorporated as an attachment to the MOU. *Answer B is the best answer.*

48. While the actions set forth in answers A and C might be taken by some negotiators, scheduled negotiations should not be changed on such short notice. If the parties are interested in building a cooperative relationship, trust is an essential quality that should be developed between the parties. Mary and Sam are the principal parties at this session and Sam should trust Mary to investigate the situation and assure the Union rights are not overlooked. Mary should assure that the situation is investigated and the promise she provided the Union actually occurs. *Answer B is the best answer.*

49. In a traditional relationship, answer A would probably occur either today or immediately after the manager implements the change. While Mary may not have the power to stop the change herself as Chief Negotiator for management, she has a Personnel Management Specialist on her team who should have the knowledge and authority to contact the manager in question or a higher-level manager to have this change delayed. If the parties are truly interested in developing a cooperative labor management relationship, *answer C is the correct answer.*

50. While the position stated in answer A might be technically correct, the establishment of a Labor Management committee is a negotiable topic. Many parties following the concepts of Partnership or cooperative relationships cite the establishment of these concepts in the negotiated agreement. However, the parties are wise to cite the concept of such an arrangement and leave the particulars to be developed through specialized training on these processes and activities of the participants involved in the cooperative relationship. *Answer C is the best answer.*

FPMI
Star Mountain, Inc.
© 2003

Using•Interest-Based•Bargaining

Chapter 5

FPMI
Star Mountain, Inc.

Using Interest-Based Bargaining

In chapter 3, we described traditional labor-management bargaining sessions. But, largely as a result of Executive Order 12871, many agencies and unions are experimenting with other ways of trying to reach agreement. Probably the most common method is called "interest-based bargaining."

This chapter describes interest-based bargaining (usually called IBB) and how it works.

After reading this chapter, you will understand:

- What IBB is and how it works

- Differences between IBB and traditional bargaining

- When IBB is likely to work and when it isn't.

Executive Order 12871

Requirements:

- Training of appropriate employees on ways of reaching agreement using techniques such as IBB

- Creating labor-management partnerships

- Bargaining on permissive topics of bargaining as defined by the labor relations statute

---

QUESTIONS

51. Sam tells Mary that the negotiations must be conducted using interest-based bargaining techniques as required by Executive Order 12871. Is this true?

A. Yes, all federal negotiations must now be conducted using IBB techniques.

B. No, it is up to the parties to decide how to conduct their negotiations.

C. Yes, it is true because either party can insist on using IBB techniques under the provisions of the Executive Order.

The • Bargaining • Book

52. Mary tells Sam that she is not opposed to using IBB to try and reach agreement on a new contract but that she thinks doing so without training their bargaining teams would be a mistake. Sam thinks she is just delaying the start of negotiations. Is Mary right?

A. No, anyone can use IBB just using common sense.

B. Based on the history between these individuals, Sam is probably right and he should press for the negotiations to start right away.

C. Sam may be right about her reasons but the negotiations are likely to be more successful if the parties have had training on how to use IBB techniques.

NOTES

ANSWERS

51. The Executive Order did not require the use of IBB techniques. It did require agencies to conduct training in "consensual methods of decision-making" which included interest-based bargaining but some problems may not lend themselves to using IBB. In short, it is up to the parties to decide for themselves how to proceed. *The correct answer is B.*

52. While Mary may be just trying to delay negotiations, her idea is a good one. Trying to begin bargaining without training when using a method different than they have used in the past may create more problems, take more time, and result in more problems. Particularly in view of the fact that the Executive Order required training on topics such as IBB, Mary's suggestion is a good one. *The correct answer is C.*

IBB Usually Involves These Steps:

• Identify problems

• Specify interests

• Develop standards to evaluate solutions

• Develop possible solutions

• Evaluate possible solutions

QUESTIONS

53. Sam and Mary have agreed to use IBB techniques on some of the issues to be addressed in their agreement. Mary suggests they swap proposals in the next 10 days on some of the more difficult issues. Sam isn't sure that is the proper way to begin using IBB techniques. Who is right?

A. Sam is right. They shouldn't be swapping proposals and developing positions if they will be using IBB.

B. There are no hard and fast rules so they can proceed any way they want to. They will just have to agree on the best way to get started.

C. Mary is right. They have to start somewhere and exchanging positions on the difficult issues is a good starting point.

FPMI Star Mountain, Inc.
© 2 0 0 3

54. Sam tells Mary he wants to start their bargaining session by having the two teams sit down together and jointly list the issues to be addressed. Then, he wants to have the two parties try and explain their concerns, if any, with the issues they have agreed on. Is this a good idea?

A. No, because one side or the other may not disclose its primary interest and may wait until later as a "surprise."

B. It won't hurt anything but this is likely to be a waste of time. They should exchange proposals to identify their concerns and then each party should explain its position.

C. This is often how IBB will actually work. Rather than taking a position, each side will identify its interests and concerns rather than defining a position.

NOTES

FPMI
Star Mountain, Inc.
© 2 0 0 3

ANSWERS

53. In traditional bargaining, the parties often exchange proposals prior to sitting down and trying to reach agreement. Interest-based bargaining is different in that the parties will often begin by identifying problems and interests with regard to that problem. In other words, neither side starts out by taking a position on an issue and trying to defend that position in negotiations.

There really aren't any hard and fast rules in the labor relations statute or the Executive Order about how to use IBB techniques. But, generally, it is much better to start by identifying problems and interests rather than exchanging proposals. *The correct answer is A.*

54. *The correct answer is C.* The term interest-based bargaining comes from the fact that each side is to identify its own interests rather than immediately taking a position and then trying to defend it.

Exchanging proposals often results in both sides defending an established position rather than jointly trying to resolve a problem. It is possible that using IBB techniques may end up being a waste of time but it is more likely that it will result in an agreement both sides find acceptable moreover arriving at an agreement will usually involve less acrimony and posturing than often accompanies traditional labor-management negotiations.

IBB Techniques

- Still require preparation

- May still result in a written agreement

- Can be used in conjunction with traditional bargaining

QUESTIONS

55. Mary tells her preparation team that the agency and union have decided to use IBB techniques. She asks this team to consider what issues they would like to see addressed in the new agreement and their major concerns. Sam hears about her instructions to her team and tells Mary she is undermining the cooperative approach to negotiations. What should Mary do?

A. There is nothing wrong with deciding in advance what an organization's primary interests and objectives are in a bargaining session. Mary is taking a correct approach.

B. Sam is right. Using IBB techniques, the problems should first be raised and addressed by the two bargaining teams; management should not be meeting by itself.

C. Mary is not doing anything illegal but her actions may undermine the union's confidence in the process. She should wait and begin preparations in conjunction with the union.

FPMI Star Mountain, Inc.
© 2003

56. While working some issues through the process of IBB, the parties find that they have a tendency to revert to position based bargaining on difficult issues. Sam explains that he was told by the National Union Representative that some parties who have more successfully used IBB have a person who facilitates the process. Sam suggest the parties consider using such a person. What should Mary do?

    A. Agree with Sam and attempt to find a person who is qualified to fill this role.

    B. Disagree with Sam since a great deal of time would be lost finding someone acceptable to both parties and training the person in IBB techniques.

    C. Suggest that the parties abandon IBB procedures for the articles that seen too difficult for those procedures.

57. After using IBB techniques to resolve several problems, Sam tells Mary he wants to reduce their agreement to writing. Mary objects because she is concerned this will create more conflict and undo what has already been done through the process. Can Sam insist on a written agreement?

    A. No, because the Executive Order did not require it.

    B. Yes, because the labor relations statute states that any agreement must be put into writing upon request of either party.

    C. No, putting an agreement in writing is contrary to the spirit and intent of the Executive Order.

NOTES

FPMI
Star Mountain, Inc.
© 2 0 0 3
The • Bargaining • Book

ANSWERS

55. IBB is quite new to most of the federal government and there are no hard and fast rules. There is nothing wrong with an agency or a union sitting down in advance with its own members to decide what their primary issues and concerns are that need to be addressed. In fact, it would usually be irresponsible not to do so. This does not mean it is necessary to develop positions, counter-proposals, etc. But an organization should understand its own priorities and objectives. *The correct answer is A.*

56. Parties using IBB often train and regularly use a Facilitator who is familiar with the IBB process and can help the parties refrain from sliding back to position based bargaining. While IBB does not always result in complete settlement of all issues, it stands a good chance of having both parties happy with the outcome of those issues resolved through this process. Parties often commit to training a Facilitator with the negotiating teams thereby building rapport between the team members and he Facilitator and assuring the Facilitator possesses the same IBB skills as the negotiators. *A is the best answer.*

57. The Executive Order did not require an agreement to be put in to writing. But the labor relations statute does require a "written document incorporating any collective bargaining agreement "resolved" if this is "requested by either party." *Therefore, the correct answer is B.*

For more indepth information on this subject you might want to obtain *"A Practical Guide to Interest-Based Bargaining"* from FPMI.

The • Bargaining • Book

FPMI
Star Mountain, Inc.
© 2 0 0 3

Impasse · Procedures

Chapter 6

FPMI
Star Mountain, Inc.

Impasse Procedures

At some point, you may reach an impasse. In the private sector, an impasse is resolved by the relative economic strength of the company or the union. If the impasse is sufficiently serious, the union will strike or the company will lock-out the employees. In the federal sector, employees cannot legally strike and the employer cannot legally lock-out employees. In lieu of economic power, the federal labor relations statute has established alternative mechanisms for resolving disputes that have not been resolved at the bargaining table.

By the end of this chapter, you will know:

• The nature and role of the Federal Mediation and Conciliation Service in federal sector negotiations.

• The nature and role of the Federal Service Impasses Panel in resolving an impasse.

• Some of the other options available to your team if an impasse is reached in your negotiations.

The Federal Mediation and Conciliation Service (FMCS)

• Helps parties reach an agreement

• Becomes involved after a request by either party or by a direct offer of its services

• Provides technical assistance to prevent disputes

QUESTIONS

58. After three months of negotiations, Mary determines that further attempts to reach agreement will be futile without assistance. She informs the union team that an impasse has been reached and that she is going to request the FMCS to provide assistance. Sam states his agreement with her conclusion that an impasse has been reached but he does not want to request FMCS assistance. Instead, he tells her that he prefers to submit the case to another third party and that the FMCS will not assist in negotiations unless both parties request help. Is Sam's conclusion correct?

The•Bargaining•Book
FPMI Star Mountain, Inc. © 2003

A. No. Management and the union must go to the FMCS first to seek bargaining assistance when an impasse has been reached. A request from both parties is not required.

B. Yes. Unless both parties request help, the FMCS will not provide assistance in the bargaining process.

C. Yes. Use of the FMCS is not required when an impasse has been reached. The parties are free to go to any third party for assistance but they must agree on the selection.

59. After several days of discussion, Sam and Mary agree to jointly request the FMCS to assist in their negotiations since agreement will not otherwise be possible. Mary prefers to have each side file a brief outlining the issues to be submitted to the FMCS for a final decision on the contents of the agreement. Sam is not sure that is such a good idea and wants to discuss it with his team first. Does the FMCS have the authority to issue a final decision on the contents of an agreement?

A. Yes, but a hearing is normally required rather than submission of each party's position through a written brief.

B. Yes, it is possible but only after the mediator has had a chance to discuss the issues with each side first.

C. No, the FMCS will only attempt to obtain a voluntary settlement between management and the union.

NOTES

ANSWERS

58. When an impasse has been reached, the FMCS is normally the third party that will attempt to obtain a voluntary settlement through the negotiations process. A mediator will lend assistance after he has determined an impasse has reached and that the intervention of a mediator may be of some benefit. It is not a requirement that both parties request assistance, as the determination of whether to provide mediation services is not always a joint decision of management and the union.

While FMCS is the required third party who intervenes in an Impasse in the Federal Government, there are some contracts that prescribe other interveners. The contracts with these provisions are few and generally were in effect for many years and fall under provisions of the Statute that "Grandfathered" these impasse provisions thereby permitting them to continue today. Your negotiated agreement would address these unique impasse proceedings if applicable.

Sam and Mary do not have the option of going to another third party agency at this point. Since they have both reached a conclusion that an agreement has not been reached and is not possible without outside help, requesting FMCS intervention is the next step in the bargaining process. *Therefore, the correct answer is A.*

59. The FMCS does not have the authority to issue a binding decision on the contents of a new collective bargaining agreement. A hearing is not held nor are written briefs filed by each side outlining a position on the issues in dispute. A mediator will use a variety of techniques or tactics to persuade the parties to reach agreement and it is through this art of persuasion that many agreements are reached at this stage of the negotiations process.

The mediator does not have a vested interest in the outcome of the negotiations and no one method of persuasion will be used. The mediator may attempt to meet with each team separately or with the teams jointly to determine any possible areas of compromise that may exist. Once a possible way to settle the dispute is sensed, the mediator may attempt to fashion a package deal wherein both sides gain and lose something they feel is important; she may attempt to persuade a team that its position is untenable for some reason; or perhaps the mediator will attempt to convince both sides not to include a particular subject in the agreement at all. The mediator does not have the authority to direct any specific agreement. In effect, if the parties decide that they will not agree on a subject, the mediator cannot force an agreement. Any agreement reached at this stage must be a voluntary one. *Therefore, the correct answer is C.*

QUESTIONS

60. Sam McLean tells Mary that the union team agrees an impasse has been reached. However, he believes the impasse would be resolved more expeditiously if the parties go directly to the FSIP rather than using the FMCS first. Can they agree to do this?

The Federal Service Impasses Panel (FSIP)

- Takes any action necessary to resolve impasses

- Determines method of resolving impasses

- Becomes involved in negotiations after an impasse has been reached

- Provides assistance when requested by either party, the FMCS, or the FSIP Executive Director

    A. Yes, as long as both teams are in agreement.

    B. Yes, the FSIP will resolve a dispute at any time either party wishes regardless of whether the FMCS has been involved in the negotiations.

    C. No, the parties must first use the services of the FMCS to attempt to reach agreement prior to going to the FSIP.

61. One of the agency team members asks Mary what authority the FSIP has to resolve disputes. What should her answer be?

    A. The FSIP has the authority to tell the parties what their new agreement will contain both as to the substance and the language of the new agreement.

    B. The FSIP can only recommend a settlement. It cannot require the parties to accept any particular settlement.

    C. The authority of the FSIP to direct a settlement or to recommend a settlement resides with the agency and the union. It only has the authority given to it by the parties.

ANSWERS

60. Under the labor relations statute, the parties may not proceed to the FSIP until "voluntary arrangements, including the services of the Federal Mediation and Conciliation Service... fail to resolve a negotiation impasse...." Therefore, it is not possible to go to the FSIP without first using the services of a mediator who is normally an employee of the FMCS. The FSIP does not consider the parties to have reached impasse until the mediator has attempted and failed to bring the parties to a voluntary settlement. *Therefore, the correct answer is C.*

61. The FSIP has the authority to take any action necessary to resolve an impasse. It can direct a settlement on both the language of the new agreement between the parties and the substance of the agreement. It will often recommend a settlement to the parties rather than direct one. If the recommendation does not resolve the dispute it will then direct a settlement.

The Panel also varies the methods used to resolve an impasse. It may hold a hearing before a factfinder; it may decide the case based on written submissions; or it can direct the parties to use an arbitrator paid by the parties to resolve the impasse. Normally, each party will have a chance to state its position on the preferred method of settlement prior to the FSIP directing the form the settlement process will take.

In short, the FSIP can take any number of steps to resolve the dispute between the parties. It also remains flexible and unpredictable as to the outcome of a case by deciding each dispute submitted on its merits and without any one case establishing a precedent to be used in subsequent cases. *Therefore, the correct answer is A.*

Impasse Options

The FSIP may approve alternate methods of resolving a dispute. Possible options include:

- Written submissions

- Hearing before a fact-finder

- Mediation-arbitration

- Interest arbitration

QUESTIONS

62. In a team meeting, Mary Jamison raises the possibility of submitting the issues remaining to interest arbitration in lieu of going to the FSIP for a decision. One of her team members questions whether this can be done. What should Mary tell him?

A. Either management or the union may request that the FSIP approve an alternative form of dispute resolution.

The•Bargaining•Book

B. The FSIP may approve a request for interest arbitration only if both management and the union concur in the request.

C. Such a request is not proper under the labor relations statute but if neither party questions it no one will ever know the difference.

63. Before the agency suggests a method for resolving the dispute, the union team suggests that the parties have the remaining issues resolved through a mediation-arbitration procedure. Mary asks Sam why he wants to use such a procedure and what mediation-arbitration really is. What should Sam tell her?

A. It is a procedure under which the parties avoid using both FMCS and FSIP to resolve the impasse.

B. It is a procedure under which a person is selected who attempts to mediate a dispute and, if agreement is not reached through mediation, the person selected will have the authority to issue a decision on the dispute that is binding on both parties.

C. It is a procedure the parties use to try to resolve a dispute before going to the FMCS or the FSIP.

NOTES

FPMI
Star Mountain, Inc.
© 2003

The • Bargaining • Book

ANSWERS

62. Interest arbitration is similar to the arbitration of a grievance as discussed in Chapter Two. One primary difference is that in an interest arbitration proceeding, the arbitrator is asked by the parties to determine the content of a new collective bargaining agreement rather than to determine how to interpret or apply an existing agreement. As the issues are frequently more complex and difficult to resolve, the cost to the parties will frequently exceed the cost of grievance arbitration.

Either party may request the FSIP to approve submission of a dispute to an arbitrator instead of having the issues resolved by the FSIP. The Panel does not have to approve such a request but is more likely to approve it if both management and the union make a joint request.

The advantages of arbitration to resolve a contract dispute are that the procedure will normally allow the parties to select the arbitrator and it may be a little faster than the normal FSIP procedures, especially if there are a number of issues still outstanding. (The Panel can also appoint an arbitrator to decide a case.) The disadvantages of such a procedure are that the process is more expensive (the FSIP does not charge for its services) and the arbitrator selected may not be as familiar with the myriad of federal requirements and procedures not applicable to the private sector or other public sector jurisdictions. *Therefore, the correct answer is A.*

63. Mediation-arbitration is a process under which a third party is selected who attempts to mediate the issues remaining to be settled. If mediation is not successful, the mediator assumes the role of an arbitrator with the authority to direct a settlement, if necessary.

Mediation under these circumstances is frequently more successful than traditional mediation because the third party (the mediator) has the advantage of the participants knowing that he can direct a settlement if they do not voluntarily resolve the remaining issues. This works because of the fear that the directed settlement will give one or the other bargaining participants less than they would get by settling. Use of the mediation-arbitration process is not common in the federal sector but has been used with increasing frequency in contract disputes where there are a large number of issues that remain to be resolved. Any use of alternate dispute resolution procedures must be approved by the Federal Service Impasses Panel. *Therefore, the correct answer is B.*

The•Bargaining•Book FPMI
Star Mountain, Inc.
© 2 0 0 3

Post-Negotiations

Chapter 7

FPMI
Star Mountain, Inc.

© 2003

The • Bargaining • Book

Post-Negotiations

What happens after the agreement has been signed? A lot of work will be wasted if the contract is signed and then abandoned by the parties and you and your team members should work to see that this does not happen. Regardless of the language in the agreement, the contract is only as good as its implementation. What are the roles and responsibilities to be played by the bargaining teams after the agreement is signed?

At the end of this chapter, you will understand:

- The role of the respective team members after the contract has been signed.

- The role of agency management in implementing the new collective bargaining agreement.

- The role of the union in enforcing the new collective bargaining agreement.

Role of the Bargaining Team

Team member should be involved in:

- Training on the new agreement

- Interpreting the agreement

- Annotating the agreement

QUESTIONS

64. After the conclusion of the negotiations, Mary mentions to the other team members that she would like to write an annotated agreement to ensure all supervisors are given the management team's interpretation of the agreement. One of the team members questions why that should be necessary since the contract should stand on its own without the team members having to spend any more time on it. What should Mary tell her team member?

A. The agreement does stand on its own and an annotated version of the agreement for supervisors is not necessary.

B. An annotated agreement can be used to show the union team how good a job the agency team did by emphasizing clauses where the union did not understand what it was really agreeing to do.

The • Bargaining • Book

© 2 0 0 3

C. An annotated agreement will assist agency management in ensuring conformity and consistency in the interpretation and application of the new agreement.

65. The new agreement provides time for the union to train the local union's stewards and officers on the provisions of the new agreement. Sam is attempting to put together a training course that includes a discussion of specific contract articles by the members of the union team during the training sessions. One of the team members tells Sam that explaining the contract should not be the function of the bargaining team because their job is done now. What should Sam tell the team member?

A. The agreement is only as good as its implementation and the responsibility of the team normally continues through the training phase to ensure that what the team agreed upon is properly implemented.

B. The training phase is important to the team because it can be used as a way to explain to the other union members the new provisions that will directly affect them.

C. The team should be involved in the training phase because it shows the officers and stewards who were not members that the agreement was a team effort and not the work of one person.

D. All of the above.

NOTES

FPMI Star Mountain, Inc. ©2003

The • Bargaining • Book

ANSWERS

64. The job of the negotiating team should not end just because the agreement has been signed. The agreement is only as good as its implementation. Management has a stake in ensuring that the new agreement is properly interpreted and applied by all of its representatives (i.e., all supervisors and management officials). Language in the agreement is inevitably going to have sections or articles that are not clear, whether or not the team intended it that way at the time the agreement was reached. An annotated agreement is simply a version of the agreement that contains guidance explaining the intent of a contract. If the agency representatives interpret the contract in different ways, the initial intent of the bargaining team may never be properly implemented. Mary should explain to her team member why his role in preparing the annotation is important. Keep in mind that joint training session with both agency and union team members may also be an effective way to explain the intent of a contract. *Therefore, the correct answer is C.*

65. Whether the team represents an agency or the union, its function is the same. Keep in mind that joint training sessions with both agency and union team members may also be an effective way to explain the intent of a contract. Sam's team member would be very useful in explaining the intent of the new agreement to employees and other union representatives for many of the same reasons that the annotation is useful to managers and supervisors. To the extent that the bargaining team can and will become involved in the training of the employees that will be using the contract, the stronger and more meaningful the new contract will prove to be in practice. In this case, all the answers given are correct. *Therefore, the correct answer is D.*

Role of Management

With a collective bargaining agreement, it is generally management's role to:

• Administer the agreement

• Ensure consistency in administration of the agreement

QUESTIONS

66. One of the supervisors in the agency has received the new agreement and has listened in the training courses as Mary Jamison and her team explained the intent of the parties on the most significant articles. The supervisor calls Mary and tells her that he disagrees with the new provision for keeping track of the time employees enter and leave the office. Because he disagrees with this provision, he tells her that he does not intend to enforce this new provision. What should Mary tell the supervisor?

A. The new contract provisions are optional and if the supervisor disagrees with them, he should not enforce them.

FPMI
Star Mountain, Inc.
© 2003

B. The supervisor has an obligation to enforce the provisions of the agreement unless he can reach an accommodation with the union by negotiating directly with the union himself.

C. The contract provisions are binding on all parties to the agreement and each member of the management team has an obligation to properly apply the contract.

ANSWERS

66. The provisions of the new agreement are binding on all members of management, the union, and the members of the bargaining unit. When the teams negotiated the provisions of the new agreement, each team obligated the people represented to live by the terms of the contract. The management team is responsible for enforcing the terms of the new agreement. The supervisor questioning Mary is not entitled to negotiate separate contract provisions directly with the union that are applicable only to his organization.

The situation posed here is not unusual and may be difficult to resolve. The agency has a right to insist that its managers and supervisors properly apply the agreement. If this is not done, the supervisor may establish new terms and conditions of employment contrary to the intent of the bargaining teams. If these terms and conditions are viewed by the union as being favorable for their unit members, the union may choose to go along with the terms and will tolerate the new practice. The result would be that the deviation becomes an established practice that management would then have to comply with, rather than complying with the intent of the agreement. If the union disagrees with the new practice, it is entitled to file a grievance to ensure proper application of the contract. In either event, what is actually implemented may not be what was intended by the contract.

While the responsibility for training the supervisors and managers on this aspect of the labor relations program lies primarily with the labor relations office, the management team can play an important role in ensuring acceptance of the new agreement and proper interpretation of the new agreement throughout all levels of the organization covered by the agreement. *Therefore, the correct answer is C.*

Role of the Union

The union polices the administration of the new agreement by:

• Ensuring proper enforcement of the agreement

• Monitoring interpretation and application of the agreement

• Representing employees in grievance

• Explaining the agreement to employees

QUESTIONS

67. One of the local union's representatives calls Sam McLean shortly after the new agreement has become effective. The representative questions the union's intent on the official time provisions of the agreement. Sam and the representative conclude that a supervisor has improperly denied the steward time away from his job to engage in union activities. The steward wants Sam to file an unfair labor practice charge against the agency to resolve the dispute. What would be the most appropriate action for Sam to take?

A. He should follow the union representative's advice and file an unfair labor practice charge.

B. He should wait until the contract expires and clarify the intent of the parties in the next agreement.

C. He should resolve the dispute through the negotiated grievance procedure.

68. Several employees have complained to Sam McLean about the agency's policy of assigning overtime. The contract language is ambiguous on the procedures to be used in assignment of overtime and the agency has not followed a consistent practice in making the assignments. What action should Sam take?

A. He should pick the case he believes best reflects the union's position and resolve it through the grievance procedure if a settlement with the agency cannot be reached.

B. As the agency has the responsibility for administering the agreement, he should let management representatives interpret and apply the agreement as they see fit.

C. He should wait to resolve the problem during the next contract negotiations.

The • Bargaining • Book

FPMI
Star Mountain, Inc.
© 2 0 0 3

ANSWERS

67. An unfair labor practice charge must allege a violation of the labor relations statute rather than a violation of the agreement. (The only exception is when there is a clear and patent breach of the contract instead of a differing interpretation of ambiguous contract language.) In this case, there is a question concerning the interpretation of the contract so filing an unfair labor practice charge would not be the best course of action.

Since the contract has just gone into effect, it would not be advantageous to the union to wait until the contract expires to attempt clarification. Most collective bargaining agreements are from one to three years long and if the issue is important to the union that is too long to wait.

The negotiated grievance procedure is designed to cover situations such as the one portrayed here when the parties are not in agreement. An arbitrator will ultimately determine how the contract should be applied when granting a union steward time away from his job unless management and union are able to reach a settlement of the grievance in the initial steps of the grievance procedure. *Therefore, the correct answer is C.*

68. Contract language is often ambiguous. Sometimes the ambiguity is intentional because it enabled the negotiators to reach agreement on an issue that could not be resolved otherwise. Sometimes, a situation arises that was not contemplated by the negotiators.

If the new situation results in a conflict, management and union may attempt to negotiate a resolution. In practice, management normally makes the initial determination as to how the contract language should be interpreted. This occurs because a situation arises and the supervisor at the worksite must decide how to handle the problem. If that decision is repeated in subsequent cases and is accepted by the union over a period of time, it becomes a condition of employment that is binding on both management and the union.

If, as in this case, the agency has not been consistent in its interpretation of the agreement, the union has an opportunity to ensure that the practice it considers the most desirable will be implemented throughout the bargaining unit. It can do this through the negotiated grievance procedure by picking the case that best represents the fact situation that is likely to result in an arbitrator finding in the union's favor.

Obviously, there is no fool proof system for ensuring that an arbitrator will rule in favor of the union or of management. However, since the union can select a case with the most favorable fact situation for presentation to a third party, this increases the possibility of the union prevailing. *The correct answer is A.*

FPMI
Star Mountain, Inc.
© 2003
The • Bargaining • Book

Effects·of·Executive·Order·13203

Chapter 8

FPMI
Star Mountain, Inc.

Effects of Executive Order 13203

On February 17, 2001, President Bush enacted Executive Order 13203 which abolished the National Partnership Council and rescinded the requirements that agencies develop labor management partnerships. As discussed in Chapter 4, the establishments of partnership councils could have occurred without Executive Order 12871, but many agencies did nothing on this issue until this EO was signed.

At the end of this chapter, you will understand:

- the effect of EO 13203 on day-to-day labor management relations
- prohibitions on maintaining established partnership councils
- political implications imposed by EO 13203

QUESTIONS

69. The agency for which Mary and Sam work had established a requirement under Executive Order 12871 that each installation with a union establish a labor management partnership. Mary and Sam led the organization of a partnership council in their installation with several managers and union representatives regularly involved in the council activities. Since the signing of EO 13203, the agency has rescinded the requirement for partnership councils. In fact, the agency directed that partnership councils be discontinued. Mary has forwarded the agency guidance to Sam. The following should happen at this point.

A. Mary should immediately prepare a letter to Sam citing the revised agency policy and notifying him that their local partnership council is immediately abolished.

B. The topic should be added to the agenda for the next partnership council meeting.

C. Mary and Sam should meet and decide the action to be taken on the agency directive since the directive states it is effective immediately.

D. Sam should propose negotiations on the Impact and Implementation (I&I) of the agency policy.

FPMI
Star Mountain, Inc.
© 2003

70. Sam is irate over the action taken by agency headquarters and wants to initiate an Unfair Labor Practice charge. His proper actions would include:

A. Filing a charge with the FLRA against Mary and local management.

B. Filing a charge with the Washington DC FLRA office against the agency since they are located in the Washington DC area.

C. Filing a charge against both the local agency and agency headquarters.

D. Contacting his union national office to determine the action they are taking.

E. Adding the topic to the next agenda of the local partnership council.

71. After establishing the local partnership council, the parties had negotiated a new Basic Agreement that established the requirement that the parties would negotiate over subjects set forth in 5 U.S.C. 7106(b)(1). This action was highly recommended by agency and union headquarters offices to satisfy the spirit of Executive Order 12871. After receiving the new agency guidance and Executive Order from President Bush, the following action should be taken.

A. Meet immediately to negotiate on changing the requirement of the Basic Agreement.

B. Management should inform the union in writing that they will no longer be negotiating over subjects covered in 5 U.S.C. 7106(b)(1).

C. They are obligated to continue to follow the terms of the Basic Agreement until it is reopened for negotiations.

D. Since negotiations on subjects set forth in 5 U.S.C. 7106(b)(1) are at the election of management, as set forth in the Statute, management can decline to negotiate each time a subject covered by this section is raised by the union.

ANSWERS

69. Executive Order 13203 was primarily effective in abolishing the National Partnership Council and many agency level partnership activities. It has effectively abolished the reporting requirements imposed by the Clinton administration and removed labor management partnerships from the spotlight in which they were focused by the previous administration. In addition, EO 13203 helped to eliminate partnership activities that were created to satisfy the demands of the previous administration and resulted in little or no relationship improvements between the parties.

Under EO 12871, the political mandate for partnership in all agencies resulted in many activities that were not genuine and were only created for the purpose of showing activity at the local level. In many of these "partnerships", very few tangible benefits were ever realized. In fact, the adversarial processes previously utilized by the parties remained unchanged. At these installations, both parties were probably happy to implement EO 13203.

In some installations, genuine partnerships were accomplished by the councils which resulted in a reduction or elimination of ULP charges and a lessening of delays in I&I bargaining since the union was involved in formulating the policies being changed. At these installations, the parties would probably follow their established procedure and discuss the requirements of the EO and the agency.

If Mary unilaterally abolished the partnership council as suggested in answer A, Sam could probably prevail on an ULP charge filed with the FLRA. The local implementation of a change in agency policy without giving the union the opportunity to initiate I&I bargaining under Section 7116(a)(5) of the Statute is generally viewed as a "bypass" of the union which results in an ULP Charge.

If the local council is effective, the proper answer to this question would be B. In many situations, effective councils have changed their names to cooperative committee, labor management discussion group, labor management committee, or other appropriate name that does not reflect the word "partnership." Other agencies simply forwarded EO 13203 without a requirement to abolish all local partnership activities. In these cases, any partnership councils that are operating effectively are continuing without regard to the Executive Order.

If the local council is effective, answers C or D would be inappropriate actions. With an effective council, Mary and Sam would never meet to discuss the action to be taken without the entire council present. The parties are free to continue partnership activities if they choose, and neither the agency nor the Executive Order can require them to change something that is permitted under the FSLMRS. If the agency requires that "partnership" activities be discontinued, merely changing the name of the council would accomplish that requirement without abolishing an effective labor management relationship.

If the local Council was ineffective, answer C would be the proper answer since both parties would likely be relieved to abolish the meaningless activity generated by non-productive meetings, if meetings were actually held. Answer D would most likely not be used in either event since the matter would normally be on the agenda for an effective council and the union would probably not be interested in preserving meetings with management if they were ineffective. However, Sam would have the right to initiate I&I under the statute.

70. Sam's reaction would be totally understandable if the local partnership council is effective. If the council is ineffective, his reaction would probably only be a ruse to further harass the agency, as some union representatives are prone to do. However, Sam only has recognition at the local level and therefore, only has standing to file an ULP Charge against local management. The agency level policy should be left to the national union, based upon any possible recognition at the agency headquarters level. If the union has national consultation rights, the national office of the union should have been consulted before the agency level policy was released. If the union has national exclusive recognition or a national agreement, the agency should have negotiated with the union on the policy before it was released.

Answer A would be appropriate if Mary proceeded to implement the policy unilaterally. Answers B and C would be inappropriate since filing a ULP against the agency should be left to the national union office. Sam would also be wise to proceed to contact the national union office as suggested in answer D. His initial actions would probably result in action under both D and E unless management unilaterally implemented the agency policy.

71. *Answer C is the correct answer.* Once the agency has agreed in the basic agreement to negotiate on subjects covered by 5 U.S.C. 7106(b)(1), that agreement must be followed until the basic agreement is again reopened for negotiations and the wording is changed, or rescinded by the agency. Failure to follow the language set forth in the basic agreement could result in an adverse finding by either the FLRA or an arbitrator, depending upon which forum the union chose to follow.

NOTES

FPMI
Star Mountain, Inc.
© 2 0 0 3

The • Bargaining • Book

Summary

Success in collective bargaining is not a mysterious process. It does require thorough preparation, a well-trained team, and a working knowledge of the rights and obligations of both management and union in all phases of the bargaining process. Most of all, it requires that each team member understand his or her role in the process; how to fulfill that role; and the confidence and planning to meet the goals and objectives of your bargaining team. *The Bargaining Book* will be useful to you throughout the entire process. Keep it as a reference source and refer to it whenever necessary.

FPMI
Star Mountain, Inc.
© 2 0 0 3

This book was rewritten and totally updated in 2002 by Philip A. Varnak who worked in the Federal Government for 32 years until he started a consulting business in 1997. In addition to performing as President of Phil Varnak Associates, Inc., Mr. Varnak is a training consultant for FPMI, primarily conducting training courses in Employee Relations, Labor Relations, Mediation, and Arbitration. He has updated two other FPMI publications, *A Desktop Guide to Unfair Labor Practices* and *A Practical Guide to Interest-Based Bargaining*.

This book was originally written by Ralph R. Smith who was co-founder and President of FPMI until his retirement in 2002. The book was taken out of print until this latest update.

FPMI Publications

- Advanced MSPB Practitioner's Handbook
- Exceptions to Arbitration Awards in the Federal Sector
- Cases in Effective Leadership
- Building the Optimum Organization for Federal Agencies: The Guide for Developing the MEO through Functionality Assessment, A-76 or Other Strategic Sourcing Study
- The Human Resources Role in Managing Organization Change
- A Practical Guide to Interest-Based Bargaining
- Managing Cyberspace in the Workplace
- Workplace Harassment: A Handbook for Supervisors, Managers, and EEO & HR Professionals
- Desktop Guide to Unfair Labor Practices
- Understanding Employee and Family-Friendly Leave Policies
- Alternative Dispute Resolution: A Program Guide
- The Federal Manager's Guide to Liability
- Managing Diversity In The New Reality
- The Federal Manager's Guide to EEO
- Supervisor's Guide to Federal Labor Relations
- The Ways of Wills
- The Federal Manager's Handbook
- Managing Diversity: A Practical Guide
- A Practical Guide To Self-Managed Teams
- Diversity: Straight Talk from the Trenches
- Face To Face: A Guide For Government Supervisors Who Counsel Problem Employees
- Customer Service in Government
- The Federal Manager's Guide To Discipline
- Win-Win Settlements: Using Interest-Based Negotiating to Resolve EEO Complaints
- Understanding The Federal Retirement Systems
- How To Build An Effective Team
- Federal Manager's Guide to Improving Employee Performance
- Career Transition: A Guide for Federal Employees in a Time of Turmoil
- Performance Management: Performance Standards & You
- The Manager's Survival Guide to Organizational Change
- Managing Effectively In A Reinvented Government
- Managing The Civilian Workforce
- The Bargaining Book
- Practical Ethics for the Federal Employee
- The Manager's Guide to Preventing Sexual Harassment
- The Federal Employee's Guide to EEO
- Managing Leave and Attendance Problems
- Working Together: A Practical Guide to Collaborative Labor-Management Partnerships
- The Federal Manager's Guide to Measuring Organizational Performance
- The Federal Employment Law Practitioner's Handbook
- The Union Representative's Guide to Federal Labor Relations

For more information on books and libraries offered by FPMI, visit the web site at http://www.fpmi.com/bk.

FPMI
Star Mountain, Inc.
© 2 0 0 3

FPMI Newsletters

• *FedNews OnLine*^{SM}
(a free daily e-newsletter covering federal issues and concerns.
Get it! www.fpmi.com)
• *Federal Labor & Employee Relations Update*
• *EEO Update*   • *The Federal HR Edge*

FPMI's e-Packages

The e-Fed® e-Package
The *e-Fed*® e-Package is a multiple-newsletter Internet-based research service. The package is affordably designed to provide agencies the tools needed in the Labor and Employee Relations, Human Resources and EEO arenas. This comprehensive package includes **all** FPMI newsletters and research services that search full-text decisions and case summaries of the FLRA, MSPB and MSPB AJ decisions.

EEO Update e-Package
The *EEO Update* e-Package is an Internet-based newsletter that provides access to summaries of significant EEO case decisions as well as significant news and features on EEO events occurring in the federal government.

Federal HR Edge e-Package
The *Federal HR Edge* e-Package is an Internet-based service that provides access to news and events affecting all federal employees and supervisors.

Federal Labor & Employee Relations Update e-Package
The *Federal Labor & Employee Relations Update* e-Package is an Internet-based service that provides articles, full-text decisions, case summaries and key points of the most significant FLRA, FSIP and MSPB cases each month.

All packages are sold through an affordable annual license that provides an agency unlimited access to this Internet service. Visit the FPMI web site at http://www.fpmi.com *for more information.*

To learn more about FPMI's newsletters and Internet e-Packages, visit the web site at http://www.fpmi.com/Newsletters/.

FPMI Products & Services

FPMI FedEd® Seminars

FPMI specializes in training seminars for federal employees, managers and supervisors. These seminars are offered as scheduled open enrollment classes or they can be conducted at your worksite at a flat rate. The instructors for FPMI seminars have all had practical experience with the federal government and know problems federal supervisors and employees face and how to deal effectively with those problems.

For more information on FPMI's seminars, visit the web site at http://www.fpmi.com/training/trainingsite.html.

Technical Services

FPMI offers consulting and technical assistance services to federal agencies in all aspects of human resources, management and EEO. With our extensive network of consultants we are ready to assist you by providing experienced professionals to perform specific tasks in virtually any human resources field — from labor relations to position classification. If you need temporary or long term assistance, we can provide you immediate expert assistance. Call FPMI to learn more about subjects covered, satisfied customers, and pricing.

For more information on the services offered through Technical Services, visit the web site at http://www.fpmi.com/.

FPMI Conferences

FPMI is known throughout the federal sector for its ability to conduct very innovative and informative conferences. Many customers refer to FPMI as the "HR Event Expert" for its ability to provide top-notch conference speakers and workshops in all areas of federal human resources. Conference subjects range from labor and employee relations topics and training to the latest human resources and managerial issues.

Customers can stay abreast of the latest information and schedules on FPMI's conferences on the web site at http://www.fpmi.com/conf.

For your convenience, you may order FPMI's products and services off the GSA Federal Supply Schedule and avoid expensive and time consuming agency procurement processes.

For more information on our products and for pricing contact:

FPMI • 4901 University Square • Suite 3 • Huntsville, AL 35816
PHONE (256) 539-1850 • FAX (256) 539-0911 • E-mail: fpmi@fpmi.com
Internet: http://www.fpmi.com

© 2003